FINDING YC
Through Grief

A Guide for the First Year

Second Edition

Marty Tousley, CNS-BC, FT

Hospice of the Valley, Phoenix, Arizona

For my son, my father and my mother, whose love for me and mine
left behind much more than death could take away.

Finding Your Way through Grief: A Guide for the First Year
Second Edition, Revised and Expanded 2008
© 1999, 2000, 2008 by Martha M. Tousley
ISBN: 978-0-9798490-3-9
All rights reserved. Printed in the United States of America.
No part of this book may be reproduced or transmitted in any form,
or by any means, without prior written permission.
Address requests for additional copies to
Hospice of the Valley, 1510 E. Flower St., Phoenix, AZ 85014.5656
602.530.6900, hov.org

This book has been printed and made available to you by the
Fabricant Family of Arizona, in loving memory of their
devoted son and loving husband.

Gregory P. Fabricant
1966-2000

Greg was a grief counselor employed by Hospice of the Valley during his short stay on earth. He was only 33 years old when he died of lung cancer. After losing his father to skin cancer, he had a most difficult time recovering from his grief, and it was then that he decided to help bring peace and understanding to others who were in need, as he once was.

After receiving his masters degree in counseling, and while working at Hospice of the Valley, he continued studying to reach his goal of attaining a doctorate in counseling/psychology.

It was his wish during his last days to continue to help people in their sad and difficult journey through the grieving process. Therefore, this book is dedicated to you, the survivor, and we hope that it will bring some solace, hope and peace to you.

"I need only say that this young man was a beloved and celebrated
prince, and that we are deeply privileged to have known him."

— Kathy Melamed, Director of Clinical Services
East Office, Hospice of the Valley

CONTENTS

Introduction

HOSPICE OF THE VALLEY BEREAVEMENT SERVICES

Hospice of the Valley offers a variety of programs and resources designed to guide bereaved family members through their first year of grief. Continuing support for the family after a death is crucial to the healing process.

Services include ongoing bereavement support groups, special focus groups and workshops for adults, teens, children and their families, short-term individual and family counseling, online grief discussion forums, periodic telephone follow-up and informal social gatherings at different times throughout the year.

In addition to a monthly calendar of events, educational material is sent to each family to help them better understand and cope with the mourning process.

Bereavement staff members and volunteers are available and will stay in touch with Hospice of the Valley families for at least 13 months after the death of a loved one. If you have questions, need information or just want to talk to someone, please contact Bereavement Services at Hospice of the Valley, 602.530.6970, or visit the Web site, hov.org.

LOSS AS A PART OF LIVING

Unfortunately, loss is one of the prices we pay for living in this world. We may like to think that life produces all gains and no losses, but deep down, we know that isn't true. Eventually, we all must leave the special places and things we've cherished, lose some of the people we've known and loved, and learn to say goodbye to them.

Few of us are prepared to face the excruciating pain associated with the death of a loved one. We think we cannot bear it, that to feel such sorrow is abnormal, as if we're going mad. We think there's something wrong with us, or something unnatural about our feelings.

Yet loss is a natural part of life's seasonal cycle of growth, decay and rebirth. When a flower blooms, its bud is lost. When nighttime comes, the day is lost. When we grow old, our youth is lost. Some losses are inevitable, some are immediate, some are sudden, and some are eventual, but they do confront us every day and are common to us all.

Some elements of bereavement are common as well: certain feelings and reactions are experienced by most people when a loved one dies. But *how* we experience them—and for how long—is uniquely personal and distinct.

As you find your way through this first year of grief, you will discover that there is no right or wrong way to do the work of mourning. There is only *your* way, and you must discover it for yourself. There is no magic formula, no short cut and no easy way out. Grief is like a long, winding tunnel whose entrance is closed behind you, and the only way out is through.

Loss creates an emotional wound, but it is an injury that can be healed. With help and understanding, the pain of loss can be transformed into a challenging new beginning, and your grief experience can become a healthy, positive and healing process.

To make the process of grief a healing one, you must go through it actively, which means moving through it thoughtfully and working with it deliberately. Expressed grief can be worked with and released, but suppressed grief will torment you in ways you cannot control. Healthy, normal mourning is a process of honestly facing the reality of your loss, coming to terms with its impact on your life, learning to access all available resources for recovery, finding meaning in your loss and continuing to live productively in the years that follow.

Every loss is a challenge to grow, but growth requires change, and change is often painful. When a loved one dies, everything changes, including you. Nothing will ever be the same again, and it may feel as if you've lost control of everything. But you will find that in fact you do have some control, especially over the choices you will make. You alone will decide whether the changes you face will be positive or negative ones. You can choose how you will respond to grief and how you will let it affect you. You can keep both your memories of the past and your dreams for the future, and you can decide not to give up on yourself and the rest of your life.

THE FIRST YEAR OF GRIEF

Death of a loved one is a highly stressful event, and the first year of bereavement can be especially intense and difficult. You must face and live through each of the four seasons for the first time without the presence of your loved one. All of the major and secondary losses attached to this death will be realized and felt anew as you confront each important holiday, birthday and anniversary, including the first anniversary of the day your loved one died. Over and over again, through an entire year's cycle of events, you may feel flooded with waves of loss and may fear that you will drown.

Many aspects of life as you knew it may be irrevocably changed: your daily schedule, your social life, your roles and responsibilities, your financial situation, your physical, emotional and spiritual well-being.

We know from working with many grieving people that certain feelings and experiences are normal, universal and predictable. This book contains useful information and practical suggestions to help you better understand and cope with the feelings and experiences of grief you are likely to encounter in this first year, to help you manage and get through what lies ahead and to offer you the hope that you can rebuild your life without the physical presence of your loved one.

Finding your way through this first year of grief takes real courage. Even as you take the first steps on your way, your destination is unclear, you don't know the length of your trip and you've no idea how long it'll take you to get there. But as you proceed, it may comfort you to remember that since the beginning of time, people have survived the most devastating losses. Whatever loss confronts you, know that you can survive. Believe that you will get through this experience, and you will not feel this way forever.

HOW TO USE THIS BOOK

Even though you must find your own way through this first year of grief—and you will proceed at your own pace—you need not travel alone. Hospice of the Valley Bereavement Services, the information in this book and many other resources are available to guide you along the way, as you learn how to mourn, to cope, to adjust and to recover from your loss.

While a book cannot protect you from loss, this one does contain useful information about the range of responses to grief considered to be normal and appropriate. It offers suggestions for tapping your own inner strength, finding the support you need, using available resources to help you cope and finding a place for your lost loved one in your own inner and social world.

Since grief reactions vary and don't appear all at once, you may not yet feel a need for certain information in this book. Depending on where you are in your grief process, your attention span may be so short that you'll find it difficult to concentrate and sometimes won't be able to absorb or remember what you're reading. Feel free to read those portions of greatest interest to you now. Then try putting this book aside, referring back to it again at different times over the next year. Reread, try on and use whatever material may be useful to you at the time.

If you are a family member or a friend of someone who is bereaved, the content of this book will help you understand what reactions are normal in grief. For example, it may seem to you that the mourner is quite off balance, especially when the first waves of shock and disbelief wear off.

The initial numbness of grief can be misinterpreted, either as a sign of indifference toward the one who died, or as denial that a death has occurred. It may give the misleading impression that the mourner is "doing just fine." In addition, the sorrow that normally accompanies grief can be misread as "depression." But more often than not, what you see in the mourner is a very normal reaction: a natural response to losing a cherished loved one. Remember that, in and of itself, grief is not a pathological condition.

Part Four of this book contains specific information that will help you know better how to respond to a person in mourning. You will find that the most precious gift you can give to those who have suffered a major loss is to be present with them in their pain and suffering. This is no easy task, as it is difficult to witness another's intense feelings of grief. But by helping the bereaved to embrace and grow through grief—to bear witness, as the pain softens and hope emerges—your own life can become fuller and more deeply lived. It is truly a privilege to walk with and learn from one who is traveling this journey, especially when you consider that grief is a matter of taking turns. One day you may find yourself on the very same path, in need of someone to be present with you in your pain, as you struggle to find your own way through grief.

Part One
Understanding the Grief Process

WHAT TO EXPECT IN GRIEF

Grief is a normal, yet highly personal, response to loss. Neither an illness nor a pathological condition, it is a natural process that, depending on how it is managed, can lead to healing and personal growth. Although the experience is unique for each individual, finding your way through it successfully will require some knowledge and understanding of the grief process and the work of mourning.

If you've had little or no experience with bereavement, you may be caught off-guard and feel totally unprepared to deal with it when it happens to you. Not knowing what to expect, you may be wondering whether your reactions are normal and dreading whatever might be coming next.

When you're armed with an understanding of grief, however, and know what feelings and experiences you can normally expect, you will be able to face the weeks and months ahead more readily.

COMMON MYTHS AND MISCONCEPTIONS ABOUT GRIEF

When someone dies, grief is felt only by that person's family members and friends.
In reality, grief is felt by anyone with an emotional attachment to the deceased, whether you know the person well or not. You may mourn for public figures you respect and admire, for example, even though you've never met them personally.

Grief is what you feel only when your loved one dies.
Grief is a normal response to the experience of loss of any kind, including unusual and secondary losses. Such grief often goes unrecognized and unacknowledged. Examples include disenfranchised losses, such as loss of a cherished pet, and losses stemming from major life transitions, such as graduation, moving, marriage or divorce, job loss, incarceration, disability or alteration in health status.

Grief is an emotional response to loss.
In fact, grief can affect us in every dimension of our being: physically, emotionally, cognitively, behaviorally, socially, financially and spiritually.

Grief and mourning are the same.
Grief is your own private, inner response to a loss. Mourning is the outward expression of grief, the social response that you openly share with others. Everyone grieves, but not everyone mourns.

Grief occurs in orderly, predictable stages.
Grief and mourning are highly individualized, according to your own unique personality and life experiences, as well as the nature of your relationship with the deceased, how the death happened, the support system you have available, your own past experience with loss and your particular religious and cultural background.

Tears are a sign of weakness.
In fact, crying at the death of a close loved one is a normal human response that is universal and occurs across cultures throughout the

entire world. Studies show that tears contain toxic chemicals created by the stress response, and crying is a natural and healthy way to release those toxins and the tension associated with them.

Medication is necessary for relieving the pain, anxiety and depression associated with grief.
Grief is not an illness to be cured, and the emotions attached to it are normal. Medication may be indicated in some cases, but the work of mourning still needs to take place. Facing grief, moving toward the pain and openly expressing what is felt on the inside is what leads eventually to healing. The normal symptoms of grief also serve as signals to others that you are in need of their compassion, patience and understanding.

Most people recover from grief and return to normal.
Grief is not an illness from which you will recover; rather, it is a gradual process of transformation. It may seem that when your loved one died, a part of you died, too. Every aspect of life is different and forever changed, and a "new normal" must be found, as you learn to integrate this loss and live in a whole new world without the physical presence of the one who has died.

Time heals all wounds, and eventually grief comes to an end.
Grief is an adaptive response that is not bound by time. It never really ends; you don't "get over" grief. It is something you will learn to live with over time, as you gradually adjust to the physical absence of the one who has died. Grief softens and erupts less frequently as time goes on, but it can revisit you at any time, and in varying intensity, whenever you are reminded of your loss.

Those who mourn are weak in their faith.
Grief often brings on a crisis in faith because a significant loss challenges all of your basic beliefs about the nature and fairness of the universe, the existence of a higher power, or even the very nature of God. Others cannot compete with this process; they need to wait with unconditional

love, patience and compassion as you find your own way and mourn in the manner that is best for you.

The first year of grief is the hardest and the time when support is most needed.
For some, the second year is even harder than the first. The reality is that you will need *ongoing* compassion and support.

The goal of grief is to let go of the one who died and move on with life.
The bonds of love are never severed by death, and if cherished memories and legacies are intentionally tended and nourished, it is normal and healthy that a close relationship with the deceased will continue and endure throughout your lifetime.

COMMON MYTHS ABOUT THE LOSS OF A CHERISHED PET

There is nothing special about the relationship between animals and humans.
Your relationship with a companion animal can be just as special and loving as those you have with any other family member or close friend. Loving an animal is different from loving a human being, because a pet loves you in a way that people cannot: profoundly, boundlessly and unconditionally.

Losing an animal is less painful and less significant than losing a human loved one.
Pain over the loss of a beloved companion animal is as natural as the pain you would feel over the loss of any significant relationship. Since cherished pets weave their way into every aspect of your daily life, in some ways, it may be even more difficult to cope with losing them. Once they're gone, you're repeatedly encountering evidence of their absence and constantly reminded of your grief.

Having close relationships with animals (and grieving at their loss) is abnormal and unnatural.

You need not let anyone influence you to believe that your relationships with animals are somehow wrong or less important than those you have with humans. Loving animals well and responsibly teaches all of us to better love all living beings, including humans. Grief is the normal response to losing someone you love, and grief is indifferent to the species of the one who is lost. Love is love, loss is loss, and pain is pain.

Relationships we have with animals are not as important as those we have with humans.

Having deeply meaningful, spiritual and healthy relationships with animals is not abnormal, and in some cases, may be more emotionally healthy, spiritually healing and personally rewarding than those we have with humans. Pets offer us a kind of loyalty, devotion and unconditional love that cannot be found in the more complicated relationships we have with relatives, friends and neighbors.

Death of a pet can be a useful "dress rehearsal" for the real thing, especially for children.

Death of a pet is often a child's first real encounter with a major loss. Suddenly friendship, companionship, loyalty, support and unconditional love are replaced with overwhelming and unfamiliar feelings of loss, confusion, emptiness, fear and grief. Far from being a so-called dress rehearsal, for most children, pet loss is a profoundly painful experience.

Most people think of euthanasia as a quick and easy way to get rid of their sick, dying, old or unwanted animals.

Deciding when and whether to euthanize a beloved pet is probably one of the most difficult choices an animal lover ever has to make. On the one hand, you know that choosing to end your animal's life will intensify your own emotional pain, yet postponing the decision may prolong your animal's pain and suffering needlessly. At such times, it is very important to explore all aspects of the euthanasia decision with your veterinarian and with others whom you trust, to listen to what your animal may be trying to tell you and to trust your own intuition.

Conducting rituals, funerals or memorial services for dead animals is a frivolous waste of time and money, and those who engage in such practices are eccentric and strange.
Whether for animals or for humans, death ceremonies and rituals help meet our needs to support one another in grief, acknowledge the important role our loved ones played in our lives, honor the memory of our departed companions and bring meaning to our loss.

WHAT YOU NEED TO KNOW ABOUT GRIEF

Grief is extremely powerful.
It can catch you totally unprepared, knock you off balance and shake you to the core. It can be painful beyond words—physically, emotionally, socially and spiritually—and it can change your life completely. Grief serves to remind you how fragile life is and how vulnerable you are to loss. It can make your present life seem meaningless and take away your hope for the future.

Understanding the process and knowing what to expect can help you cope.
Your pattern of progressing through your grief will be uneven, unpredictable and unique, with no specific time frame, but the more you learn about grief, the better you can cope with it. In the beginning, it will seem as if your grief is running you, but in the end, you can learn to run your grief. When you understand what is happening to you and have some idea of what to expect, you will feel more in control of your grief and will be in a better position to take care of yourself, to find your own way through this loss and to begin rebuilding your life.

The worst kind of grief is the grief you're experiencing now.
Don't compare your grief with anyone else's, and know that, at this moment, your loss is the worst thing that could happen to anyone. Acknowledge that your loss is worthy of grief. Where there is loss, there is grief. Pain is pain. Accept that you must endure the very real feelings of sorrow.

Grief work is very hard and takes enormous energy.
Much as you may want to do so, there is no way to avoid this grief of yours. You cannot wait it out; you won't get over it quickly, and nobody can do it for you. It's called grief work because finding your way through grief *is* hard work, and if you put it off, like a messy chore, it will sit there waiting to be done. And the longer it waits, the harder it becomes.

Effective grieving is not done alone.
Unfortunately, friends and family members may be finished with your grief long before you are finished with your need to talk about it, and unexpressed feelings can become distorted. It is important that you find an understanding, non-judgmental listener with whom you can openly acknowledge your feelings and experiences, express and work through your pain and come to terms with your loss. If friends and family aren't as available as you need them to be, or if your need exceeds their capacity to help, consider contacting Hospice of the Valley Bereavement Services (602.530.6970), whose caring office staff, volunteers, bereavement counselors and support groups stand ready to help you.

How grief is expressed varies among individuals.
Everyone grieves differently according to their age, gender, personality, culture, value system, past experience with loss and available support. Grieving differs among members of the same family, as each person's relationship with and attachment to the deceased family member varies. How you will react to this death depends on how you've responded to other crises in your life; on *what* was lost when this death happened (not only the life of the person who died, but certain aspects of your own life as well: your way of life; who you were in your relationship with that person and who you planned to be; your hopes and dreams for the

future); on *who* died (spouse, parent, child, sibling, grandparent, relative, friend or other; how you lived together and what that person meant to you); on the person's *role* in your family; on *when* the death occurred (at what point in the life cycle: yours, as well as that of the person who died); and on *how* (the circumstances surrounding the death and how the death occurred).

Certain manifestations of grief are typical, common and normal.
Although grief is as individual as you are, some feelings and reactions are universal. Their intensity will vary, and they'll happen in no particular order. You may experience all, some or none of them; they may happen only once or many times, sometimes several years after your loved one's death. Respect your own feelings and reactions. Take time to look, listen, experience and understand them. They are nature's way of getting your attention.

Grief is a lifelong process.
Perhaps the most commonly asked question in bereavement is "When is grieving finished?" While the agonizing pain of loss diminishes in intensity over time, it's never gone completely. It is absolutely normal to feel the aftershock of loss for the rest of your life. Grieving is not a reaction to a single event, like an illness that can be cured and from which you will recover. It's more like a deep wound that eventually heals and closes, but whose scar remains and still can hurt at times.

Grief changes through the years.
It changes you, as well, influencing who you are in the present and affecting who you'll become in the future. It must be worked through, adapted to and integrated into your life, as different situations will require you to accommodate this loss again and again. You will re-visit the event continually as you grapple with its meaning—emotionally, socially, economically and spiritually—and as you struggle to find a place for your dead loved one in your present and future life.

Death may have ended your loved one's life, but it did not end your relationship.
The bond you have will continue and endure throughout your lifetime, depending on how you take your memories and your past with you into the future. Many grievers report maintaining an active connection with their deceased loved ones by talking to them, dreaming about them, sensing their presence or feeling watched over and protected by them. It is normal and healthy to foster these continuing bonds, as you decide how your loved one will be remembered, memorialized and included in your family and community life.

Time does not heal grief.
Time is neutral. It is not the passage of time alone that heals. It is what you *do* with time that matters. Grieving is an active process, not a passive one, and recovery is a choice. You can learn how to use this grieving time to help you heal yourself.

ANTICIPATORY GRIEF AND MOURNING

Grief does not wait for death to happen; it occurs both in *anticipation* of and *following* a loss. Extended illness, disability, severe accidental injury, a terminal diagnosis or the aging and decline of an elderly family member can produce what is known as *anticipatory grief and mourning*. You are reacting and continually adapting not only to an expected loss, but to *all* the losses—past, present and future—that are encountered in that experience.

Anticipatory mourning begins as soon as you become aware that death *may* happen. It begins when a life-threatening illness is diagnosed or a terminal prognosis is given, you understand that there is no cure and realize that death is likely or inevitable.

Issues of grief and loss are inherent in the care giving process, and grief is experienced by everyone involved, whether you are the patient grappling with the illness or disability, or the family member, partner, close friend or care giver who is intimately connected with and looking after your loved one. You are coping not only with your own feelings of grief and loss, but also with physical and mental fatigue, and you may feel overwhelmed with all the financial, legal, medical and personal responsibilities associated with care giving.

In some ways, anticipatory mourning can be harder than the grief you experience after the death, because when you are waiting for the death to happen, you are on constant alert, living in a state of emergency over an extended period of time.

On the other hand, this period offers the benefit of preparation time, as you and those close to you begin to think about your life without the one who is dying and how you and your loved one can use the time remaining to reflect, prepare for the future and finish unfinished business.

Suggestions for coping with the anticipated death of a loved one:

- Recognize that, in the beginning, it is normal to feel shocked, dismayed, helpless and numb, especially if the onset of the illness is sudden or unexpected. You need time to take in this most unwelcome news, at a pace that is tolerable for you.

- If you have the time and the skills, use the Internet to research the latest developments concerning the illness. List medical specialists conducting studies or research on the disease or condition. Locate local support groups related to the illness.

- Investigate and reach out for available help and community support. Assemble a team of family, friends, clergy, neighbors, colleagues, health professionals, home health care and housekeeping services, church and other volunteer organizations. Explore care giving resources on the Web, such as those listed at www.griefhealing.com/care-giving-links.htm.

- Contact Hospice of the Valley or your local hospice at any time to inquire about hospice services. It is not necessary to wait until treatment aimed at cure is replaced with the goal of comfort and symptom relief. The best time to learn about end-of-life care is well in advance, when educated decisions can be made based on the input of everyone involved. The hospice staff will contact your doctor to determine if and when a referral to hospice is appropriate. Alternatively, you can talk with your loved one's doctor directly, and he or she can make a referral to hospice.

- Have emergency phone numbers and important resources readily available (legal, insurance, medical, financial, home repair).

- Identify what needs to be done, and find help to do it (errands, grocery shopping, household repairs and maintenance, transportation, housecleaning, prescription pick-ups).

- Follow the lead of the person who is dying, as a unique individual experiencing illness in a personal way, and choosing whether to openly discuss the illness and impending death.

- Encourage, but do not force, open, honest communication among caregivers, family members, friends and the one who is dying. Recognize and respect the fact that some individuals may not be able or willing to talk about the reality of the illness and its probable course, either at the present time or with certain other persons or family members. Know that it is natural to take in the reality of a terminal diagnosis gradually, as facing it all at once is overwhelming. Listen without judging, giving others permission to express their thoughts and feelings about the illness without fear of criticism. Let others know how you are feeling and what you need.

- Remember that this time for warmth, sharing and togetherness will not come again. Although communication may be frustrating and painful, now is the time to contemplate and clear up unresolved issues—to say, do and share what is especially intimate and meaningful, in a positive, affirming and encouraging manner.

- Allow for the expression of difficult feelings by using alternative communication tools, such as letters, video or audiotapes.

- Anticipate the family's new reality after the death, and do what you can to help the dying person complete end-of-life tasks (last will and testament, distribution of possessions, funeral preparation, gathering and safeguarding important documents, such as medical, legal and family papers).

- Expect changes in the ways family members interact with one another. As the illness progresses, roles will shift. Responsibilities formerly held by the dying person will be reassigned, and everyone must adjust to those changes. Maintaining some of the normal family routines will help to provide security in the midst of all the chaos.

- Let some details slide. Slow down, and focus on what is most important. Remember that the emotions that seem to have taken over your life right now will not last forever, and the rest of your life will not seem so sad and overwhelming.

- Practice good self-care. Pay attention to your family's needs for adequate rest, nutrition, exercise, recreation, respite and fun. In your efforts to remain strong and care for the dying person, don't let your own physical, emotional and spiritual needs, or the needs of other family members (especially children), get lost or neglected. Keep a journal or a diary, seek individual counseling, find and participate in an in-person or online support group for care givers.

- Embrace and express your spiritual beliefs, if faith is important to you and your family. Turn to those spiritual practices that bring comfort, peace and hope: prayer, meditation, listening to your inner voice, reading, attending religious services. Recognize that, under these circumstances, it is not at all unusual to feel angry at the doctors, at the one who is dying, or at God for the injustice of it all. If there are some things you prefer to discuss with someone outside the family, talk with a pastoral counselor or spiritual advisor. Find someone you trust who will not judge you and who will listen to whatever thoughts and feelings you may need to explore.

What if the one who is dying is a child?

- Give yourself time to confront the harsh reality that, as unfair and unnatural as it seems, the child is terminally ill and will not recover. Parents do not expect to outlive their children; it goes against the natural order of things. It is extremely difficult to process and accept the fact that a beloved, innocent child is dying.

- Follow the child's lead. Listen first, and do what you can to support and encourage open and honest communication with the child and among family members. Answer only what is asked, but be meticulously honest, using language at the child's level of development and understanding. Lying to children in an effort to protect them from the truth of their condition is neither respectful nor loving, and can lead to confusion, frustration, mistrust and anger.

- Pay attention to questions, statements or behaviors that may suggest a child's trying indirectly to communicate other needs, questions or concerns.

- Help the dying child live, laugh and play as happily and as normally as possible. Spend as much time together as you can. Help to maintain relationships and contact with peers through play dates, visits, phone calls, letters, cards and e-mail.

- Remember the needs of the dying child's siblings.

- Do what you can to support and nurture other family members and close friends.

- Find and utilize all available sources of support (Hospice of the Valley, Make-a-Wish Foundation, Candlelighters Childhood Cancer Foundation and others).

Suggestions for coping with grief immediately after the death:
It has been said that experience is not what happens to you, but rather what you do with what happens to you. So it is with grief. Now that this death has happened to you, you must decide what you can do with your grief. Coping with grief is not a passive process; it involves many courses

of action, and throughout this book, you'll find a number of suggestions for coping. Let's begin with these:

- Know that you're not losing your mind; you are grieving.

- Believe that you will return to your normal level of functioning.

- Give yourself permission to operate at half speed right now.

- Be patient with yourself; grief takes time.

- Read some accounts by other mourners for assurance that your reactions are normal.

- Slow down if your thoughts are racing and you feel as if you're running from one task to the next.

- Keep in mind that it will all get done, and not everything must be done today. Make a list, then prioritize it.

- Put off whatever big decisions you can, until you can think clearly and until you can adjust to a new and different life.

- Deal with one concern at a time.

THE EFFECTS OF GRIEF

Grief does not occur in easily defined stages; it is more a blend of emotional, cognitive and behavioral responses. Death of your loved one will affect the whole of you, body and soul. Over the next 13 months and beyond, both your initial and later reactions will be felt and expressed in each of these dimensions: physical, emotional, social and spiritual.

PHYSICAL REACTIONS TO LOSS

When the stress of an emotional injury is felt, there will be warning signs in the body. Expressing emotional pain indirectly through physical symptoms may be more acceptable in some families and more worthy of attention, but it is very hard on the body and it can be dangerous. When you don't express your emotional pain directly, your body may do it for you.

Grief can cause any of these physical symptoms:

- Low energy: needing more rest, tiring more quickly, feeling generally fatigued.

- Hyperactivity: an intense state of arousal or panicky feeling, bursts of physical energy, difficulty sitting still, needing to move around.

- Crisis response: elevated heart rate, high blood pressure, muscle tension, dizziness, weakness, headaches, not feeling well, tightness in the throat and chest, shortness of breath, dry mouth, feeling overwhelmed.

- Susceptibility to illness: suppression of the body's immune system.

- Aggravation of pre-existing chronic medical conditions or precipitation of new ones: ulcers, colitis, hiatal hernia, arthritis, asthma, migraines, back pain.

- Sighing or yawning: shallow breathing, inhaling frequently, trying to catch your breath.

- Feeling off balance, uncoordinated.

- Nausea.

- Temporary hair loss.

- Internalizing, or taking on symptoms of the illness your loved one had.

- Erratic eating and sleeping patterns: insomnia, weight loss or gain; susceptibility to the abuse of drugs, alcohol, nicotine, caffeine and food; heaviness, feeling as if you're made of lead; feeling "out of sync" with your body; distorted perception of time and distance.

Caring for yourself won't erase your grief, but it will offer a welcome respite from it. Pampering yourself with "food for the soul," such as a massage, manicure, pedicure, facial or bath, releases body tension and makes you feel nurtured. Even though your energy is low and you don't feel like establishing a healthy routine, force yourself to do it anyway. Pay careful attention to your need for nutrition, rest and relaxation, exercise and human contact.

Nutrition can suffer because appetites often shift after loss. In an effort to comfort and nurture yourself, you may eat more than usual, or you may have trouble eating anything at all. Stress can interfere with the absorption of important nutrients, while fats and sugars deplete energy.

Rest and relaxation are essential. Because rest relieves, restores and refreshes you, it is important that you make time in your day for "mindless" activity, or get away for a relaxing weekend. Your usual sleep pattern may be disrupted in the first few weeks of grief. You may not sleep well at all, or you may sleep more than usual as a way to avoid or shut out the pain.

Exercise is good for you, since regular physical activity stimulates the release of biochemicals in your body that relieve pain, alleviate stress and enhance your sense of well being. Exercise increases your circulation, stimulates your heart, cleanses your body, discharges negative energy and gets you out and about.

Human contact is a basic human need. Touching, hugging, holding and having contact with another is comforting and healing.

Suggestions for coping with physical symptoms:

- Ask someone to stay with you to help you focus and prioritize what needs to get done.

- Inform your physician what's happening in your life, so your blood pressure, weight changes and other health indicators can be monitored.

- Know you will make it through these episodes, even if it doesn't feel like it at the time.

- Recognize that your thinking processes, coordination and reaction time aren't up to par right now.

- Breathe. Frequently throughout the day, stop what you're doing, take a deep breath, hold it, then exhale very slowly.

- If your diet is not well balanced, try supplementing it with vitamins and minerals. Add fruits, vegetables and grains. Eat smaller, more frequent meals, rather than three big ones. Eat foods you like that are easy to fix and digest, and include a special treat now and then.

- Drink plenty of water.

- Find an exercise you can do (stretching, walking, swimming, dancing, swinging or swaying to music), and set aside time to do it regularly.

- Reach out and touch someone. Cuddle children and pets, hold hands with your friends, get a massage.

- Attend to personal grooming (hair, skin, nails, wardrobe) that will enhance your body image. There is truth in the saying that when you look good, you feel good, too.

If you're having trouble sleeping, try using the methods recommended by accredited sleep centers:

- Cut back on your caffeine and nicotine intake several hours before going to sleep.

- Exercise regularly (for at least 20 minutes, three times a week).

- Avoid self-medicating with drugs or alcohol, which can offer only temporary escape, have serious side effects, affect motor coordination and mental acuity, lead to dependency, magnify feelings of depression and disrupt patterns of sleep.

- Use sleeping aids only as prescribed by your doctor and only as a temporary way to break the cycle of sleeplessness.

- Condition yourself to fall asleep to guided imagery, using pre-recorded audio programs with soothing music and voice tones.

- Avoid going to bed hungry or after a heavy meal late in the evening.

- Drink a cup of warm milk or water at bedtime (plain milk is a natural sedative).

- Separate yourself from the stresses, worries and distractions of the day (yesterday, today or tomorrow). Wind down by reading, or taking a relaxing bath or warm shower before bed.

- If your spouse is the one who died, sleep on your spouse's side of the bed; it's easier if your own side is empty.

- Put on a night light, but keep your bedroom as cool, quiet and dark as possible.

- Maintain a consistent sleep-wake cycle. Stick to a regular routine; retire and get up at the same time each day, even on weekends.

- Avoid naps lasting longer than 30 minutes, especially after 3 p.m.

- Establish a bedtime ritual. Cue your body to slow down and relax by preparing for bed the same way each night, and go to bed when you are sleepy.

- Follow a deep relaxation routine; perform deep breathing exercises in bed.

- Listen to music that soothes your soul and decreases tension.

- Visualize being in your most favorite and pleasant place.

- Associate your bed only with relaxing, sleeping and sexual pleasure— don't use it for other activities that can initiate or stimulate worries and concerns.

EMOTIONAL REACTIONS TO LOSS

Shock

When you sustain a sudden and severe injury, nature's initial reaction is to send your body into a state of shock. When you're hit hard with an emotional injury as severe as the death of a loved one, it is just as natural for you to shut down emotionally and turn off inside. It's as if the magnitude of the loss, the fact that your loved one is gone forever, is too much to take in. As you begin to absorb what's happened, your brain goes on automatic pilot. Somehow you do what needs to be done, but it feels as if you're just going through the motions, like some sort of robot or automaton. There's a sense of unreality, as if you're watching yourself in a movie or a having a bad dream. You may feel frozen, numb, stunned and disconnected, unable to feel anything. You may be short of breath, confused and feel unable to cry or to speak.

Suggestions for coping with shock:

- Realize that shock is nature's way of cushioning you against the full impact of loss. It's a temporary protective mechanism that allows your mind to catch up with the brutal reality of death. Like an emotional anesthetic, it numbs the pain and enables you to move through the funeral and some of the other tasks you must complete in the initial days of mourning.

- Understand that as the numbness subsides, you will begin to experience more fully some of the other grief reactions as they emerge. This can happen days, weeks and even months after the death.

- Expect the numbness to wear off gradually, as you mobilize your inner resources and gain the strength you need to accept and absorb the reality of the death. How long this takes will vary, depending on your individual characteristics and your situation.

- You may find yourself dreaming about the person who died, forgetting your loved one is gone, or thinking you've seen, smelled, heard or touched the person. This is your unconscious mind trying to undo what happened, to re-write this unacceptable story.

- Realize that others may misinterpret what's going on with you and may conclude that you're stronger or feeling better than you really are on the inside.

- Don't feel you have to maintain a brave exterior. Holding onto your emotions takes more energy than releasing them.

- Acknowledge your own need for safety and try to find it. For example, ask a friend to stay with you if that is what you need.

- Allow others to nurture you. Lean on them, physically and emotionally, and ask for the specific help you need.

- If you don't feel up to sorting through and distributing your loved one's clothing and other belongings, it's all right to wait until you're ready.

- Be patient with yourself. Experience whatever comes without criticizing yourself.

- Take an active part in planning and participating in your loved one's funeral, memorial service or other ritual of remembrance.

- Make no major decisions about your future life.

- If questions about your loved one's illness or death arise after the shock wears off, go ahead and ask them, even if they occur to you months or years afterward.

- The more you review the details of the death, the more real it will become for you. Ask friends to let you do this, as often as you have to, and if they need a break to tell you so. If your need is more than they can handle or endure, seek help from Hospice of the Valley Bereavement Services.

Difficulty making decisions

The first few hours following a death are usually filled with turmoil and disruption. Relatives, friends and neighbors are constantly ringing the doorbell and calling on the phone. You will be faced with all sorts of immediate decisions, such as making funeral and travel arrangements, and less urgent ones, like dealing with finances and legal matters.

You may have to make some painful adjustments to your lifestyle. You may have to give up travel or retirement plans, move into a smaller house, live on a tighter budget or take a job. If you're in a state of shock and not at your best, it is wise to postpone major legal, financial and housing decisions, at least until you can discuss them with a trusted relative, friend or financial advisor.

Help with immediate tasks
Friends and neighbors can assist with immediate tasks, such as housekeeping, preparing food and answering the telephone and doorbell. They also can notify others of the death, shuttle people to and from the airport, or host those from out of town.

Making major decisions
Professionals, such as your funeral director, family attorney, financial advisor, tax accountant and insurance agent, can be valuable guides to help you make major decisions. If you're having trouble remembering everything you're being told, take notes. Whenever you speak with an official about legal or financial matters, make a brief note of the conversation, including the person's name, the date and a brief summary of what was said, so you'll be able to refer back to it if you need to.

The complexity and expense of settling the estate depends on its type and size. The services of an attorney and a tax accountant usually are helpful. Sometimes the personal representative named in the will can handle estate matters. Information on how to handle probate cases typically is available on the Web site of the court that has jurisdiction over those matters. (In Maricopa County, view: www.clerkofcourt.maricopa.gov/ filing_counter.asp)

If you want to hire a lawyer to assist you, get referrals from friends or consult the local bar association for an attorney specializing in wills, estates and probate. It is wise to discuss fees beforehand. Take the will to the attorney for review. If there is no will, the attorney will instruct you as to how to proceed.

In order to settle your loved one's affairs and to establish claims for benefits, you'll need to locate certain documents. Look for them in your loved one's safe deposit box, brief case, home and office desks, safe, locker, shoe boxes, cedar chest or file cabinets. Always keep the originals in a safe place, and for now, don't throw anything away.

Be aware that you will need more than one copy of the death certificate. Proof of the death is the one basic document you'll need to settle the estate, to establish benefit claims and to have your loved one's name removed from accounts. Make certain that you ask for an ample number of certified copies, since the raised seal verifies its validity and legality. You can ask for your funeral director to obtain copies of the death certificate for you, or you can check the local records division listed in the phone book under Government and Community Services.

Inform credit card companies and banks of your loved one's death; find out if the outstanding balances are covered and how to file a claim. When you contact the company, office or agent who insured your loved one's life and health, ask for claim forms and instructions on how to file them. Submit any outstanding medical claims to the proper insurer.

Notify banks at which your loved one had accounts. Immediately set up a new account to handle funds received after the death. Inform employers and business associates. Benefits may include employee group insurance policies, retirement and pension fund benefits, the monetary value of commissions and wages or credit union balances. Ask if you are eligible for health care coverages, for how long and at what cost. If your loved one lived alone, you'll need to notify the post office, utility companies and landlord, if any.

In addition to Social Security, you may be eligible for other benefits, depending on where your loved one worked. Social Security benefits are not automatically paid after a death; you must contact your nearest Social Security offfice (ssa.gov) to apply for them.

For Civil Service benefits (survivor's annuity), file with the U.S. Office of Personnel Management (opm.gov). For Veterans benefits, file with the U.S. Department of Veterans Affairs (va.gov). If a spouse served in the military, benefits include funeral expenses, an American flag for the casket, burial at no charge in a national veterans' cemetery area, dependency and indemnity compensation payments, potential pension payments and educational financial aid assistance.

With whatever benefits you obtain, make no decision under pressure or duress. Take time to evaluate your financial situation and seek counsel from your financial advisors. Be aware that you may feel guilty for receiving money when your loved one dies, and you may feel the urge to spend it as soon as possible. If you don't need all the money right away, investigate the different settlement options and choose the best one for your situation.

Moving to a different home
In deciding whether moving from your present home is necessary or desirable, these are some factors you'll want to consider:

- Housing costs should be limited to 30% of your income.

- Staying where you are offers the comfort and security of being in your own familiar surroundings, if that is financially practical.

- Moving away may depend upon work and educational opportunities for you and other members of your family. Think about location and transportation, in terms of convenience and proximity to resources.

- Moving in with relatives can be pleasant, convenient and economical—or it can be restrictive, stressful and in conflict with your own lifestyle and philosophy.

Money matters
If you stand to receive a substantial amount of money in the form of an inheritance or insurance settlement following your loved one's death, consider these precautions:

- Avoid making hasty decisions. If you feel compelled to a make a quick decision to sell property, move away, liquidate assets, lend money to friends or family members, or buy what you don't need, you may be your own worst enemy. Here's a good rule of thumb: *Make no major decisions for at least six to 12 months after the death, until you've experienced all the seasons of your emotions.* You are especially vulnerable right now and not in the best frame of mind. Money *does* matter, now and for your future! Focus on caring for yourself. If making decisions is unavoidable, get the best advice you can find. Until you're emotionally able to make decisions you won't regret later, try making ones that are reversible (taking a leave of absence instead of quitting your job; renting out your home rather than selling it; visiting with family for a week or two before deciding to move in; taking a long vacation away from home before deciding to move permanently).

- Watch out for obituary chasers. Certain companies and individuals watch obituaries, wait a month or two until the settlement is finalized, then contact the survivor with a so-called opportunity of a lifetime. Trust those you know instead of strangers!

- You are not a bank. When so-called "good friends," long-lost relatives and other freeloading types suddenly appear out of nowhere, remember that you are not a bank, and you need not let others treat you like one! You are wise to keep your financial situation to yourself.

Disbelief and denial

For weeks, months, or even years after the death occurs, the shock of loss may continue in a wave of disbelieving aftershocks. The process is a gradual one of weaning and disconnection. "Forgetting" that your loved one is gone, you may find yourself setting an extra place at the dinner table, expecting your loved one to walk in the door at the usual hour, or be on the other end of the line when the telephone rings. And each time it happens, you're confronted once again with the brutal reality that your loved one is forever gone. Denial is a defense against that brutal reality. It blunts the impact of the loss, offers you a temporary respite and allows you to process those overwhelming feelings more gradually. On one level, you recognize that your loved one has died; on another level, you're unable to grasp all the ramifications of that reality.

Denial is a problem only if it is used deliberately to avoid the reality of death or to escape the emotions resulting from a loss, which can manifest themselves as insomnia, fatigue or chronic depression. You may be avoiding reality to one extent or another if you:

- Continue to speak of your lost loved one in the present tense.

- Refuse to believe your loved one has died.

- Pretend the deceased is away on a trip.

- Leave clothes and other personal articles just as they were for months after the death and get very upset if anyone moves them.

- Dispose of anything and everything that serves as a reminder of the deceased.

- Neither talk of the deceased, nor speak your loved one's name.

- Downplay your relationship with the deceased.

- Stay so busy with work or travel that you are running away from your grief.

- Resort to chemicals (drugs, alcohol, nicotine) to block out the pain of loss.

Suggestions for coping with denial:

- Understand that denial serves a normal function, especially in the beginning. It is your mind's way of protecting you from more pain. Besides, your brain doesn't "get it" because it is loaded with memories of your loved one. Although the person has died, the one you love continues to exist in your memory and in the memory of others.

- Your goal is to acknowledge the truth and accept the reality that your loved one is dead.

- Denial must be dissolved eventually, but there's no specific time frame. It becomes a concern only if it interferes with your ability to function normally.

- Don't pretend that things are all right when they are not. Be honest with yourself and others. Distractions may keep you occupied, but don't help you move toward resolution.

- Face up to the truth of your pain; open up the protective shell you've built around yourself.

- Take a hard look at what is gone and what remains. Take stock, count, recite and recount what's been lost.

- Face the fact of the death squarely. Name it, spell it out and talk it out. Replace delicate words and phrases, such as *passed on* and *passed away,* with more truthful terms like *died, dead* and *widowed.*

- Try some confrontations and experiences to jolt yourself out of your denial. Confront the reminders, rather than avoiding them—both pleasurable and painful: people, places and situations. View your loved one's body, visit the grave site, reread old letters, smell a favorite cologne, look at photographs, go to church, listen to songs, gather meaningful sayings and phrases, visit special places, wrap yourself in your loved one's clothing.

- Let others (especially children) see your tears and participate in your sorrow; it lets them know how much you care and assures them it's all right to feel sadness when you lose someone you love.

Mystical experiences

Of all the various ways that grief can express itself, perhaps one of the most unsettling is to experience the presence of a lost loved one days, weeks or months after the death has occurred. When one so dear to you is gone, it can be very hard to accept that the person is really dead. You may find yourself thinking and dreaming about your loved one much of the time, and it may seem that everything around you is a reminder of the person you have lost. Once in a while, you may temporarily forget that your loved one is gone, and you'll look and listen for him or her—and maybe even think that you've seen, heard, smelled or touched the person. Part of you *believes* your loved one is there, yet the other part of you knows that's *not* the case. At some point, you may think you've received a symbolic communication or message from the person who has died. Some people find this to be very frightening and disorienting, while others find it to be quite helpful and even comforting. In any case, it's important to know that such experiences are very *common* and perfectly *normal* during times of loss. Sometimes, as long as a year after the death of a loved one, people will report sensing (hearing, feeling, seeing) the person in the room. They *believe* the person is there, yet they also know their loved one is dead. They may feel very foolish or embarrassed—they may be very frightened—and they often wonder, "Am I going mad?"

No one knows *why* grief produces such powerful, mystical processes, but we *do* know that hallucinations, communications, dreams, visions and visitations are a frequent experience of the bereaved. They are by no means abnormal, and they do *not* forecast a complicated grief reaction. While some people find them distressing, it is generally believed that such mystical grief experiences have great power and personal significance for the mourner and may be an important, if not vital, part of healing.

Suggestions for coping with mystical experiences:

- Make use of your dreams: record them, or share them with someone who will listen, but not interpret them, for you. Keep in mind that no one is a better expert at interpreting your dreams than you are.

- Don't judge yourself or others who have mystical experiences, and don't think there's something wrong with you if you've never had them. Grief responses differ from one person to another, and it is normal to experience a wide range of emotions during the grieving process.

- Don't worry whether such experiences are real or simply a figment of your imagination. If they bring you comfort, does it really matter? And if such an experience is unpleasant or frightening for you, make certain that you talk to someone who will support you.

Confusion, disorientation and fear

As the fog of shock and denial begins to lift, you will find yourself headed into the very heart of grief, and you'll become painfully aware of how very much you have lost. An entire gamut of feelings washes over you in overwhelming waves of sorrow. You are flooded with intense, raw feelings of anguish, sadness and fear, as you realize that life will never, ever be the same. You may be flooded with questions, too: Why did this happen to me? How will I be able to go on? How will I be able to face the future without this person? When will I get myself together? You may be flooded with bittersweet memories: all the things you would have, could have, or should have said and done and now will never be able to say or do. You may have difficulty concentrating and remembering and feel incapable of making the simplest decision. You may experience nightmares, dreams and phobias. You may fear that you're going crazy and may even want to die.

Suggestions for coping with confusion, disorientation and fear:

- Know that it's normal to ask such questions, and you need not expect to have all the answers. Asking such questions can be the beginning of dealing with loss.

- When you feel anxious or afraid, recognize this as a natural part of the mourning process. Your confidence in yourself and your sense of safety in this world have been shaken by this death.

- Be gentle with yourself; don't push yourself too hard, and don't expect too much. Remember that you are physically and emotionally vulnerable now.

- Take some time off if you can.

- Surround yourself with helpers. If there are others who can take care of details and help you get through the rituals of death, let them do so. If you prefer to be alone, say so.

- Focus on your own survival, and take it one day at a time.

Anger

You may not feel angry at all, since anger isn't part of everyone's experience. Nevertheless, when you're frustrated and hurting, it's only natural to lash out and look for someone to blame. Being angry is a way of channeling energy, of making some sense of the pain. When you are protesting an unjust loss, you may have every right to be angry. Even if you know your anger isn't logical or justified, you can't always help how you feel. Emotions aren't always rational and logical. Feelings are neither right or wrong, good or bad. They just *are,* and for some of us, being angry may be preferable to feeling the underlying hurt and pain of loss.

You may find yourself feeling angry:

- At yourself for what you did or failed to do, whether it is real or imagined.

- At your loved one for dying and abandoning you.

- At a surviving family member for not being the one who died.

- At medical or nursing staff who expressed little or no sympathy during your loved one's illness or death.

- At the doctors or the health care system for failing to save your loved one.

- At the situation which suddenly rendered you helpless and powerless, when all this time you thought you were in control of your life.

- At fate or at God for letting your loved one get sick and die.

- At life because it isn't fair.

- At the rest of the world because life goes on as if nothing's happened, while all *your* dreams are shattered and your life's been turned upside down.

- At others who have not lost what you have lost; who aren't suffering; who are more fortunate than you and don't even see it or appreciate it; who cannot understand what you are going through; who will go back to their lives as usual.

- At others for being happy (part of a couple, part of an intact family) when you are not.

Anger is a powerful emotion that can be frightening, but feeling angry doesn't necessarily imply that you will lose control or take your anger out unfairly on others. Before you can get through it, let go of the intense emotions attached to it and move on, your anger must be admitted, felt and expressed, if only to yourself. When you simply acknowledge feelings of anger to yourself or a trusted other without actually doing anything about them, no harm is done, to you or anyone else. On the other hand, if anger is suppressed and held on to, eventually you may erupt like a volcano, internalize it and take it out on yourself (in the form of depression or anxiety), or misdirect it toward innocent others such as family, friends and colleagues.

Suggestions for coping with anger:

- Recognize what you were taught about anger as a child and how that may affect the way you experience and deal with anger now.

- Seek to understand what's driving your anger, resentment or disappointment. Examine whatever expectations you had of others that were not met. What did you expect that did not happen? Were your expectations reasonable? Were others capable of doing what you expected?

- Discover ways to discharge the energy of anger in appropriate, non-destructive ways that will bring no harm to yourself, to others or to property. Find a safe place, space, activity and time where you can let your anger out through:

  › Physical exercise: sports, brisk walking, pounding pillows, chopping wood, digging holes, scrubbing floors.

  › Hobbies and crafts: painting, pottery, stitchery, woodworking.

  › Music: blowing a horn, pounding drums or a piano.

  › Writing: keeping a journal, writing a letter and tearing it up.

›   Talking: finding someone you can talk to, without feeling judged or being told you're bad because you're angry.

›   Reaching out: asking others for the support you need, rather than expecting them to know.

▪ If you've decided your anger with another is justified, you can choose to deal with it by:

›   Confronting the person constructively with what happened and how you feel about it.

›   Realigning your expectations, accepting the person's limitations and seeking the support you need elsewhere.

›   Leaving the relationship.

▪ If you think you're in danger of hurting yourself or someone else, if you're feeling as if your anger is out of control, seek professional help at once.

Guilt

Even if there is no basis for it, we often feel guilty for what we did or didn't do, said or failed to say when our loved one was alive.

Guilt is a normal response to the perception that we've somehow failed in our duties and obligations or that we've done something wrong. It generates a whole mixture of feelings, including doubt, shame, inadequacy, insecurity, failure, unworthiness, self judgment and blame, anxiety and fear of punishment.

When your loved one's terminal illness was finally diagnosed, you may feel guilty that you hadn't noticed symptoms sooner, waited too long to seek treatment, or didn't do enough to comfort him or her. If death came suddenly or unexpectedly, you may feel guilty for not being present when it happened. If it came after a long, lingering illness, you may feel guilty for feeling relieved that your loved one's suffering is over and you're now free from the burden of worry and care. You may feel guilty that you are the one who survived, or uncomfortable that you received an insurance settlement or inheritance following the death of your loved one. If you're a religious person, you may feel guilty that you feel so angry at God.

Unfortunately, guilt is a natural and common component of grief. When someone you love dies, it's only human to search for an explanation, to look at what you did or did not do, to dwell on the what ifs and if onlys. You agonize and tell yourself, "If only I'd done something differently, this never would've happened." Sometimes, though, there simply *isn't* anything you could've done differently. When your loved one's illness or death occurred, chances are that whatever happened beforehand was not intentional on your part. Given the stress you were under then and how exhausted you may have been, you were doing the best you could. Given the information available to you at the time, you were doing what you normally would have done. Harsh as it may seem, consider that even if you *had* done things differently, your loved one still could have died in some other way at some other time! Sometimes, we act as if we can control the random hazards of existence, even when we know that death is a fact of life.

Guilt is driven by our own personal beliefs and expectations, and dealing with it requires that we examine what we think we did wrong, face it and evaluate it as objectively as possible. For example, what did you expect of yourself that you did not live up to? Were your expectations unrealistic? If they were, then you need to let go of them. Since you did all that you were capable of doing at the time, there simply is no basis for your guilt, and you need to let go of that, as well.

Nevertheless, if after careful examination of the facts, you find that your expectations of yourself are legitimate, and you still did not live up to them, it's important to face and take responsibility for what you believe you could've done differently. Healthy guilt allows us to own up to and learn from our mistakes. It gives us a chance to make amends, to do things differently next time, to come to a better understanding of ourselves, to *forgive* ourselves and move on.

Suggestions for coping with guilt:

- Identify what it is that you feel guilty about. Resist the urge to keep such thoughts and feelings to yourself like so many deep, dark secrets. Bring them out into the open where they can be examined. Share them with a trusted friend or counselor who can view your thoughts and feelings more objectively and challenge what may be irrational or illogical.

- Listen to the messages you give yourself (the *should haves, could haves* and *if onlys)*, and realize the past is something you can do absolutely nothing about.

- When guilty thoughts come to mind, disrupt them by telling yourself to *stop* thinking such thoughts. Say **"Stop!"** firmly and out loud if you need to.

- Live the next day or next week of your life *as if* you were guilt-free, knowing you can return to your guilty feelings any time you wish. Pick a start time, and stop yourself whenever you make any guilt-related statements.

- Write down your guilt-related statements, set a date and pledge that from that day forward, you won't say them to yourself anymore. Post them and read them every day.

- If you are troubled by feeling relieved that your loved one's suffering has ended, know that a heavy burden has been lifted from your shoulders. You have been released from an emotionally exhausting and physically draining experience, and to feel relieved is certainly understandable.

- If you believe in God or a higher power, consider what He or She has to say about forgiveness.

- Participate in a support group. It's a powerful way to obtain forgiveness and absolution from others.

- Be your own best friend. What would you have said to *your* best friend if this had happened to that person? Can you say the same to yourself?

- Remember the good things you did in your relationship with your loved one and all the loving care you gave. Focus on the positive aspects: what you learned from each other, what you did together that brought you joy, laughter and excitement. Write those things down, hold onto them, and read them whenever you need to.

- Ask what you expected of yourself that you didn't live up to. How is it that you didn't? What were the circumstances at the time? What have you learned from this that you'll do differently next time?

- What can you do to make amends? Find a way to genuinely apologize to your loved one's spirit, and ask for forgiveness.

- Have a "visit" with your loved one. Say aloud or in your mind whatever you didn't get to say while your loved one was still living. Be as honest as you can be.

- Ask what it would take for you to forgive yourself. Can you begin doing it? Say out loud to yourself, "I forgive you." Say it several times a day.

- Remember that no one else can absolve your feelings of guilt. Only you can do so, through the process of forgiving yourself.

- When you've consciously learned all you can learn from this situation, and when you've made any amends you consider necessary, then it's time to let go of your guilt, to forgive yourself and to move on.

- Channel the energy of your guilt into a worthwhile project. Do good deeds in your loved one's honor.

Sorrow

Although feelings of hopelessness, anguish and despair are normal following any major loss, the intensity and duration of those feelings will vary from one person to the next, as the reality of the loss becomes more apparent in daily life. The sorrow of grief saps your energy, making even simple tasks like getting out of bed in the morning, tending to personal grooming, fixing a meal or going somewhere with friends seem overwhelming and exhausting. You may feel negative and critical toward everything and everyone, including yourself. Even in the company of others, you may still feel lonely and prefer to avoid gatherings of any size.

You may find yourself crying at the slightest provocation or at unexpected moments. On the other hand, you may fear that if you show your sadness, there will be no end to it, that if you permit yourself to cry, the tears will never stop. As a child, you may have been taught that crying is a sign of weakness, and strong people (especially men) don't cry. If it is the style of some in your family to be strong and silent in front of others, you may have to accept it and allow for it. Nevertheless, it is far better to let the tears come, and welcome them as a natural and helpful form of release. When you permit yourself to let go for a time and release what you feel, you'll be better able to function afterward. In addition, get rid of the notion that you're crying too much; there is no such thing. It is physically impossible for anyone to cry 24 hours a day. Let others (especially children) see you cry. It shows them that you care deeply about the person who died and reassures them that it's all right to express sad feelings in front of others.

You may have the pessimistic belief that things will never get any better, as if life and living are useless. Thoughts of suicide are not unusual when you're grieving. It is difficult for you to imagine life without your loved one, and you may feel a compelling need to join or to be with the person who has died. Nevertheless, there is a vast difference between thinking about suicide and acting upon such thoughts. In grief, thoughts of suicide are usually fleeting and reflect how desperately you want the pain of loss to end.

It's important to note that the sorrow of grief is not the same as clinical depression. A griever looks outside and sees the *world* as poor and empty, while a depressed person looks inward and sees the *self* that way. Depression is a treatable illness. If you're concerned that you may be depressed, consult with your doctor, bereavement counselor or clergy person. You may need medication or counseling, or you may need only to be reassured that your feelings are within the normal limits of grieving.

Suggestions for coping with sorrow:

- Expect these feelings of sadness; know that they are normal and they will pass.

- Put yourself on a regular daily routine, and set goals that are manageable and achievable. Take baby steps, rather than giant ones.

- Schedule activities you enjoy, knowing you will feel moments of sadness, as well as pleasure, and accept both sets of feelings without guilt.

- Resist the urge to be all by yourself. Find someone you can trust who will listen to your pain.

- Try setting aside a certain *crying time* each day when you can deliberately immerse yourself in grief. Use triggers and props to help bring on your tears (music, photographs, writings, sad movies).

- Avoid the use of drugs and alcohol, which may add to your feelings of depression.

- Find a support group.

- *Seek professional help* if after a reasonable period of time, despite everything you've tried to do, you still feel no relief from these feelings. If you feel you are "coming apart," no longer in control, isolated with no one to turn to; if you are turning to alcohol or drugs to cope with stress; if you feel hopelessly depressed; *if you feel suicidal,* contact someone immediately. If a trusted friend, relative, clergy person or counselor is unavailable or unable to help you right now, choose another option:
  - › Dial "0" or 911.
  - › Call the National Suicide Prevention Lifeline, 1-800-273-8255.
  - › Call the National Suicide Prevention Center Hotline, 1-800-784-2433.

SOCIAL REACTIONS TO LOSS

Loneliness and solitude

With an overwhelming sense of missing the person you've loved comes the crushing awareness of all that you've lost. You'd give anything to be together again, if only long enough to be relieved of your loneliness and to be reassured that your loved one is still a part of your life.

At other times, you may feel a need for solitude. You'll *want* to be by yourself, to get away from other people and withdraw temporarily from the pressures and decisions of daily life. This need to turn inward, to reflect on your loss, to get in touch with your innermost feelings, is common and not to be feared. In fact, it can be a helpful time for you to find your tears and figure out where you are going from here.

Isolation from others

Our culture isn't comfortable with the subject of death, and few of us know how to cope with the pain of loss and grief. We don't permit or encourage the free expression of sorrow. Instead, we learn to control our feelings and hide our pain so we won't disturb other people. As a child, you may have learned that grief is a taboo subject, that feelings should be buried and that grieving should be done alone. As an adult, you may equate grieving with self indulgence or self-pity. You may be too embarrassed or ashamed to let your emotions show in front of others. You may feel isolated, different and apart from everyone else, convinced that no one understands, and you must grieve alone. You may feel stunned at the normalcy of life around you as people go about their business, totally unaware that *your* world has stopped, and your entire life has been turned upside down.

You may be reluctant to turn to others, either because you haven't learned to accept or ask for help, or because you're afraid others won't know what to do with your feelings. If they're unfamiliar with the intensity and duration of grief, or uncomfortable with the expression of strong emotions, they may offer only meaningless platitudes or clichés, change the subject, or avoid you altogether. And there may be times when you will feel hurt by thoughtless, trivializing comments such as: *It was God's will; I know how you feel; Life must go on; Count your blessings; You must be strong for your children; It could be worse;* or *At least she/he had a good life.*

Some people you know may be done with your grieving long before you are, expecting you to be "over it by now" or worrying that you're somehow "hanging on" to your grief. Uncomfortable with your strong feelings, they may change the subject or avoid any mention of your loved one's name.

Suggestions for coping with loneliness and isolation:

- Think about who is supportive to you in your environment and what gives your life purpose and direction (family members, pets, relatives, friends, neighbors, co-workers, teachers, colleagues, clubs, athletic activities, groups, church groups, support groups, bereavement counselors). With whom are you most comfortable, and who is the most comfortable (accepting and caring) with your grief? Look for those who will listen without judging you, or for those who have suffered a similar loss.

- Find time with others to talk, to touch, to receive support. Be honest with others about what you're feeling. Allow yourself to express your sadness, rather than masking it.

- Don't expect others to guess what you need. When you want to be touched, held, hugged, listened to or pampered, say so.

- If all you want from others is help with simple errands, tasks and repairs, say so.

- Let others (especially children) know if and when you need to be alone, so they won't feel rejected.

- Go somewhere and have a good, long cry, and do it as often as you wish. You have every right to miss the person who has died. Accept your feelings as normal.

- Find time alone to process what's happened: to remember, to dream and to think.

- Identify your loneliest times, and think of how you can alter your routines and environment. For example, rearrange the furniture in a room; plan your weekends ahead of time; use your microwave for quick, easy meals.

- While some folks really are thoughtless and don't think before they speak, bear in mind that many well-meaning individuals have yet to experience a significant loss, so they really don't know what grief feels like, how to respond, or what to say. They aren't deliberately trying to hurt you. You can choose to bear with such people, you can enlighten them about what you know of grief, or you can look to others who are more understanding to find the support you need.

- Realize that no one can totally understand the relationship you had with your loved one.

- Ask people to remember, talk about and share stories about your loved one with you.

- Become more aware of how your own usage of words affects other people. Rather than saying something hurtful, admit that you don't know what to say.

- Consider getting a companion animal (which can be a wonderful source of unconditional love), but only after you've investigated what kind of pet would suit you and your lifestyle.

SPIRITUAL REACTIONS TO LOSS

Regardless of one's identification or affiliation with an organized religion, spiritual doubts and questions may arise when a loved one dies. Suffering a major loss usually causes us to confront and re-think our basic beliefs about God, religion, death and the afterlife. Some may turn to God as a source of strength and consolation at the time of a loved one's death and find their faith has deepened. Others may question the religious teachings they've practiced all their lives and find the very foundations of their beliefs shaken to the core. Even those who had no religious upbringing at all may still feel abandoned by God or angry with God for letting their loved one get sick and die. Not all people respond to loss in the same way, and not everyone shares the same cultural, religious or spiritual beliefs about death and the afterlife.

Death forces us to confront the spiritual questions we may have been avoiding or haven't taken time to address, the questions that get at the very heart and meaning of life: Who am I? Why am I here? Where am I going?

Whether a strong religious faith will be a help or a hindrance in your recovery from grief depends on what you believe and how your beliefs are practiced. Like any other resource, religion can be used in healthy, appropriate ways, or it can be abused in unhealthy, inappropriate ways.

Religion can influence your fundamental view of life: you can see life as temporary and death as permanent, *or* you can see it the other way around—death is temporary and life is permanent. Death may interrupt a life that was very special, but it cannot cancel the relationship. Religion can provide the motivation required for grief recovery: It says you're not alone, somebody has done it before. Grief's path isn't a dead-end street; it's a well-marked trail. Religion can be a great antidote for the loneliness that accompanies every major loss, and it can be a source of strength and group support. It can help you make some sense out of those basic spiritual questions about life and death, and it can help you move through the grief process more effectively.

What religion cannot do is give you immunity from loss or give you back your lost loved one, nor can it provide you with a shortcut through grief. In his book *Life After Loss,* pastoral counselor Bob Deits identifies some religious beliefs that can have a negative impact on mourning:

- Death is God's will and should not be questioned.
- The person was so special that God called him or her to be with Him.
- There must be a grand plan or purpose (a *why*) for every death.

These religious beliefs may be more helpful:

- This is a mortal, frail, imperfect world, and tragedies occur.
- There is *no* satisfactory explanation when loss occurs.
- The question is not *why me,* but rather *if me,* what can I learn from this?

Deits encourages moving from *why* questions to *how* questions:

- How can you work through this loss and achieve as full a life as possible?
- How can you use this experience to help someone else?
- How do you find meaning in life without this person?
- How do you start anew?

Suggestions for coping with spiritual reactions:

- Recognize that a new faith can grow from grief into a deeper, more mature understanding of the divine dimension of life. Sometimes, meaning must be lost before it can be found.

- Consider talking to a chaplain, minister, priest or rabbi. Pastoral counseling can comfort you and help you find a pathway to renewed faith.

- Make space in your schedule for daily meditation or prayer, which can be a source of great strength and consolation.

- Explore and question the values and beliefs you've accepted in the past, and formulate new ones when you need to.

- Consider grief as an encounter with life's greatest mysteries: the meaning of life; the promise of rebirth; the depth of love we share with one another.

Part Two
Managing Your Grief

EXAMINING YOUR OWN ATTITUDES, BELIEFS AND ATTRIBUTES

As you wrestle with your grief, it may help to think about other times in your life when you've been in the midst of a crisis or confronted a major loss. How did you cope with the situation? Did you try to ignore what was happening? Busy yourself with work or other matters so you wouldn't have to deal with it? Lose control of your emotions and "fall apart?" Or did you engage in active problem solving? Look to others for information and support? Learn from the experience and develop new coping skills?

To a greater or lesser degree, and depending on age and experience, we each have certain attitudes, beliefs and personal attributes that can help us through the mourning process.

Suggestions for coping:

- Realize that you have faced major changes before and that you have grieved, recovered and gone on. Expect that you will recover from your grief this time, and know that it is possible.

- Remind yourself often that you will not always feel the way you do right now. The pain won't last forever.

- Live one day at a time, and if that's too much, break it into even smaller chunks.

- Take it easy. New responsibilities can wait. You already have enough work to do.

- Maintain as regular a routine as you can. When you don't even feel like moving, it will help you get from here to there.

- Pace yourself. Grief bombards your system with stress-related chemicals, and you need occasional relief from them. Take a break; go for a walk; play with your pet. Give yourself something that offers refreshment and diversion. Your grief will still be there when you come back, but you'll feel better able to deal with it.

- Educate yourself about the grief process. Your grief will feel safer and more predictable, you'll understand yourself better, and you'll feel less "crazy" and afraid. Read and learn about bereavement through articles, books, audiotapes, seminars, workshops, classes and groups. Such activities expose you to models of survival and growth and give you hope that you can make it, too.

- Look at the attitudes that direct your life, be willing to re-examine old, long-held beliefs, and discard what is no longer effective and life-enhancing.

- Recognize, embrace and develop your own personal strengths:

  › *Courage* to experience and face the feelings of grief in spite of your fear.

  › *Patience* to let grief run its course, however long it takes.

  › *Resilience* to bounce back from stress and go on.

  › *Perseverance* to lean into the pain and stay with the suffering, having faith that you will endure it and get through it.

  › *Perspective* to step back from the intensity of your feelings and view what's happening from a distance.

  › *Humor* to be able to take your pain less seriously, if only for a moment.

- Check your progress along the way. Every few months, take time to assess where you are compared to where you've been. Pay attention; notice signs of improvement however small, and reward yourself for your efforts.

MINIMIZING STRESS IN YOUR LIFE

Recognizing the major sources of stress in your life is the first step in developing effective coping strategies. You need good physical and emotional health to help you mobilize your inner resources, successfully negotiate the grieving process and overcome the barriers you'll encounter. Researchers have shown that the more life changes we experience within a short time, the more likely we are to get sick or sustain an injury. The higher your score on a scale rating major life events, the harder you should work to stay well. One way to do that is to monitor and reduce to a minimum the number of changes happening in your life, such as marital separation, retirement, job changes, beginning or ending school, or moving. No one can take your stress away completely, but there is a lot you can do to minimize its harmful effects.

Suggestions for coping with stress:

- Keep it simple: Simplify your life; look for simple pleasures.

- Do it now: Do only what needs to be done right now, and let it be enough.

- Don't procrastinate: Get the necessary, unpleasant tasks over with quickly and move on.

- Learn to say no or not now.

- Avoid stressful situations: Leave the room, go for a walk, choose not to go.

- Boost your self image: Dress in clothes that make you look and feel good.

- Maximize your chances of success: Make hard tasks as easy as possible; break big ones into smaller ones; bring a friend with you; build in a reward.

- Be gentle with yourself and others: Try not to be so perfect, to do so much, to please others at your own expense. Recognize that this is a difficult time for all family members. Give each other space and support.

- Don't set yourself up for a bad time: Minimize your exposure to uncomfortable or difficult situations and people.

- Keep your expectations of yourself and others realistic: Be flexible. Ask how much it really matters, and do only what's within your capabilities.

- Breathe! Get more oxygen to your brain by breathing deeply, slowly and from your abdomen, not your chest.

- Let off steam: Find a physical outlet for your anger and frustration. Punch a pillow; pull weeds; sweep the patio; sit in your parked car with the doors and windows shut and scream.

- Don't sweat the small stuff. After what you've lost, it's all small stuff.

- Laugh! Reinforce your sense of humor; release your body's natural pain killers. See a comedy, read a joke book, listen to Garrison Keillor on Public Radio, or watch tapes of classic television shows like *Carol Burnett* and *Johnny Carson.*

- Remember past successes when you experience a setback or defeat.

DOING THE WORK OF MOURNING

It is when denial falls away, when you begin to recognize and experience most intensely all the reactions to your loss, that the real work of mourning begins. In ways that are personal and unique to you alone, you will gradually integrate your loss into the framework of your life, as you slowly give up the reality that included the physical presence of your loved one.

If you've ever worked out on a regular basis, you know that it requires a great deal of time, effort and commitment, but when done consistently over time, it produces physical, emotional, mental and spiritual benefits. So it is with grief work. Doing the work of mourning takes enormous energy. It is both emotionally and physically exhausting and may well be the hardest work you'll ever do, but it also can produce tremendous healing and growth.

Much as you may want to forego this labor, whatever issues you don't address will lie there, waiting to be resolved. When feelings are expressed outwardly, they can be released. When they're held onto, they just fester and keep on hurting.

The work of mourning can be done through private activities, such as reading and writing and with others through talking, participating in bereavement counseling, or finding support in a group. It is an active rather than a passive process, not only of coming to terms with your loss, but finding meaning in it as well, so both the painful experience of your loved one's death and your life without that person will count for something.

Suggestions for coping with the work of mourning:

- Believe that there is both a purpose and an end to the work that you must do, and trust that you'll find your way through this grief.

- Take responsibility for doing your own grief work. The decisions you make, the feelings you feel, the tears you cry belong to you alone, and no one else can do your mourning for you.

- Take time out and time off whenever you need to do so. Your grief will be waiting when you return.

- Ask for help when you need it, from others who understand the grief recovery process, or who are working through losses of their own.

- Take all the time you need. Grief work will take more time and effort than you ever thought possible, but you will make it through this.

Personal ways of expressing grief

Because grief is an intensely personal experience, your personal grieving style will be unique to you and your individual personality. You may find it helpful to return to activities of self-expression that satisfy or relax you, or discover new ones that bring you comfort and relief, such as walking, hiking, playing golf, fishing, meditating, writing or journaling, engaging in hobbies (carpentry, gardening, photography, collecting) or arts and crafts (painting, drawing, modeling, woodworking), listening to or making music, or simply talking and crying.

Writing is one of the oldest methods of self-exploration, self-expression and self-discovery. An ongoing workbook, diary or journal can be a trusted friend, available to listen to you at no cost, 24 hours a day, regardless of what mood you're in. It accepts whatever you have to say, from the ordinary to the profound, and never chastises you for what you said. You might try using a three-ring or spiral notebook, rather than a bound journal so special that you'll never want to write in it. Write as often as possible, but not as a chore. Once you get your pen moving, your thoughts will follow. You might begin with a meaningful quotation you found or a thought you want to remember.

Writing offers you the opportunity to:

- Reflect on the meaning and significance of death in your life as it applies to your inner self.

- Write your feelings down as a map of your journey toward healing.

- Separate and sort through all the confusion and conflicting emotions that surface after a loss.

- Obtain the relief that comes when you can express your thoughts and feelings and know that you have put them down somewhere.

- Awaken your memories.

- See in your writing, in black and white, what's happening inside yourself.

- Pay closer attention to your life.

- Let off steam, release tension and express creative urges in a safe and harmless way.

- Develop a deeper understanding of yourself and others.

- Clarify what you're thinking and feeling, as you move from thinking to writing it down.

- Alleviate any concern about losing your ideas and thoughts, since you'll have them for further reflection.

- Make room for new avenues of thinking, as you leave space inside you for other thoughts.

- Express yourself in complete privacy, since this writing is for your eyes only. This is not for public consumption, nor is it meant to be a "finished" piece that requires neatness, precision, good grammar, correct spelling and complete sentences.

Suggested topics for writing:

- A narrative of whatever thoughts, feelings and observations may enter your mind.

- A composition: a poem or story, a prayer or psalm.

- Drawings or other visual materials (dreams, fantasies, diagrams).

- Illustrations, clippings from magazines, newspapers.

- Personally meaningful quotes you've read or heard.

- "Bright ideas" for brainstorming all possible alternatives to problems.

- An inner dialogue (imaginary conversation) between yourself and your loved one.

- A conversation with your dead loved one, taking both parts.

- A letter to the person who died expressing thoughts and feelings, such as:

  › A special memory you have about the person.

  › What you miss most about the person and your relationship.

  › What you wish you'd said or hadn't said.

  › What you'd like to ask the person.

  › What you wish you'd done or hadn't done together.

  › What you've had the hardest time dealing with.

  › Ways in which the person will continue to live on in you.

  › Special ways you have for keeping your memories of the person alive.

Identifying a personal support system

Reaching out to others is often very difficult when you're struggling with grief, but the more support and understanding you have around you, the better you will cope. You may wish that others would just be there for you without your having to ask, but that's not likely to happen. It's not that they are uncaring; there simply is no way for them to fully understand the significance of your loss and the depth of your pain. Inform your family, friends and co-workers about what's going on with you, and let them know what they can do for you that will help. People aren't going to know what you need from them unless you first figure out what you need and from whom, and let them know directly and specifically. If they've never experienced a major loss and know nothing about grief, invite them to read this book, especially *Part Four: Helping Another in Grief,* so they'll have a better understanding of what you're going through.

Suggestions for identifying a personal support system

- Identify the *people, groups and activities* in your life that form your personal network of support and help give meaning to your life. Consider asking a friend or family member to help you develop a more complete listing, especially if you don't have the energy to do this by yourself. Write down each potential source of support, including their name, telephone number and address, so you'll have them handy when you need them. *People* you can depend on might include family members, relatives, friends, neighbors, teachers, colleagues, clergy, your family physician, family lawyer, accountant, insurance agent and Hospice of the Valley bereavement staff. *Groups* might include your church community or your affiliation with work or special interest circles, clubs, organizations and Hospice of the Valley bereavement support groups. *Activities* could include:

› Listing all the interests, activities, hobbies, courses or skills you've enjoyed in the past or always wanted to pursue, and following up on at least one of them each week or each month.

› Visiting your public library or local bookstore and asking for information, literature, films, audiocassettes and videotapes on grief, bereavement and loss.

› Finding local chapters of national self-help and support organizations related to your specific type of loss.

› Watching and listening for announcements of lectures, workshops and seminars on grief in the community. Check local radio and television stations, newspapers and bulletin boards in your grocery store, library, church or school.

- If you have a computer and access to the Internet, use the keywords "grief" and "grieving" and visit one of the many sites on the Web that offer information and support to people who are grieving, such as GriefHealing.com.

- If you work outside your home, let your supervisor or employer know what's happening in your life. Assure them that although you may not be at your best right now, you have every reason to believe that in time, your performance will return to normal.

- If you need information on bereavement groups, classes and workshops offered at various times and locations throughout the Valley, if you have questions, or if you just need to talk, you can always call Hospice of the Valley Bereavement Services: 602.530.6970.

Finding support in a group

Friends, family members and co-workers may not fully understand or appreciate the attachment you have with your loved one and the pain you may still be feeling weeks and months after the death. What is more, your need to talk about your loss may outlast the willingness of others to listen. So later in your grieving, a support group may be one of the few places where you can come to be among others who understand and where you can still talk about the one you have loved and lost.

It's important to note that group support is not the same as group therapy. Support groups aren't meant to cure long-standing emotional problems, alter people's personalities, or change their basic values or beliefs. Neither are they just social gatherings designed to introduce people of similar interests, although friendships may develop outside the group as members get to know one another.

As the name implies, a bereavement support group forms a healing circle that helps members bear up under the heavy burden of loss without giving way. The group provides a safe, structured place where normal, healthy people bound by the experience of loss can come together on a regular basis to share their stories, have their concerns and feelings validated, learn more about the grieving process, express and work through their feelings, and reflect with one another on the meaning of it all. Members have the opportunity to grow by giving help, as well as receiving it.

Most support groups are facilitated by people who have lost loved ones themselves, worked through their own grief and are committed to helping others get through the experience. Although some groups have the added assistance of a professional bereavement counselor who can offer expertise and educational information on grieving that may not be available otherwise, the facilitator's role is the same: to provide structure and to make certain that everyone in the group feels safe.

What goes on in a support group meeting will vary with its leaders, its membership and what is shared, but typically the facilitator starts by stating the purpose of the group and its "ground rules." For example: Group begins and ends on time. Information shared in the group stays there. When outside the group, members aren't free to talk about another member by name without that member's permission. Members can exchange telephone numbers if they wish to do so. Members may share as much or as little as they so choose. A person who isn't ready to talk can "pass." One person speaks at a time. Everyone gets equal time to share, so no one monopolizes the time. Suggestions may be offered, but unsolicited advice is not given. One by one, people then are invited to introduce themselves and to tell as much or as little of their stories as they wish. Experiences, thoughts and feelings are openly expressed, and painful, as well as pleasant, memories are recalled. Oftentimes, photographs of loved ones are passed around. Sometimes poems, eulogies, or tributes are read, but whatever is shared is held in the strictest confidence by everyone there.

Depending upon where you are in your grieving process, you may not feel the need for a support group just yet, but that may change over time. There is no right or wrong time to come to a meeting, but if you decide to do so, you might try coming to several meetings, rather than just one, since each one changes depending on the composition of the group and what is discussed in it. Once you've found a support group, make certain it's made up of grievers with whom you can identify, whose facilitator is not only comfortable running support groups, but also knowledgeable about the grieving process.

Hospice of the Valley provides ongoing bereavement support groups at various times and locations throughout the Valley. If none of these groups fits with your schedule, the bereavement staff will help you find alternatives offered by others in the community. Please call Bereavement Services for further information: 602.530.6970.

Finding support online

If you have access to a computer with an Internet connection, you have at your fingertips a wealth of grief information, comfort and support. Using online chat rooms, discussion forums and message boards, you can even connect with and share your experiences with others whose losses are similar to your own.

In addition to "in-person" support groups, Hospice of the Valley also offers its own online *Grief Healing Discussion Groups*, at www.hovforum. ipbhost.com. Selecting from more than a dozen individual forums, mourners with similar losses can network, mourn together and support one another in their own safe, healing place. Forums range from general issues of bereavement to specific types of loss, including that of a spouse or partner, a parent, child, sibling, or even a cherished pet. Bereaved teens have their own separate forum where they can gather and communicate with one another.

The service is available at no cost, at any hour of the day or night, seven days a week. It is safe and confidential. Membership is free and simply requires registration with a unique user name and secret password of one's own choosing. Forums are moderated by professional bereavement counselors, and individual messages are monitored for appropriateness.

Members participate when they wish and are able to, not at a set time, which can be an advantage for those whose schedules won't permit their attending an in-person support group. Participation can be especially helpful on anniversary dates, celebration days and holidays.

When one member posts a message, anyone can respond with love and caring to the thoughts and feelings of an individual, and other readers can benefit from the information shared. Whether reading or posting and responding to messages, participants come to a greater understanding of each other's grief and loss, as everyone becomes more caring, accepting and tolerant of one another. One benefit is that those members who post have an ongoing, written record of all the responses they've received, as well as access to all the other messages and responses posted on the site. By comparing more recent posts with older ones, individuals can track their own progress over time. New members witness the growth and positive transformation that occurs among more seasoned members, which gives them hope for their own future.

In addition, such a service:

- Enables you to be interactive at a time when it is difficult to interact in normally social ways.

- Allows you to express feelings, ask questions and get responses in a reasonable amount of time, usually within a matter of hours.

- Gives you practical information about the grieving process in general.

- Enables greater understanding of your own reactions to a particular loss.

- Assists in resolution of your grief.

- Enables sharing of your experiences and discussion of your feelings, without fear of being judged.

- Reassures you that what you're going through is normal, that you are not alone and that other mourners know your pain, even if friends and family do not understand.

- Offers nourishment and protection in a safe environment that awakens the natural healing process.

- Informs, directs and gives you access to other valuable resources, links to grief-related articles, stories, poems, inspirational writings, pamphlets, magazines, books, videos, sites, centers, organizations, remembrance pages and memorial sites.

- Provides information to help you be more supportive of friends, neighbors, family members and others who are also in mourning.

Before you decide to participate in any online grief forum or message board, consider these precautions:

- Investigate before you participate. Notice whether the service is sponsored by a reputable organization, and learn whether the moderators are qualified to offer information and support.

- Read about the moderators to learn about their background, education and training. Make sure they have experience in facilitating groups and knowledge about the normal grief process. Read some posts written by the moderators to get a sense of their approach to grieving people.

- Make certain that the group or forum you select is made up of mourners with whom you can identify. Read some of the posts in a forum to decide if you can relate to the people gathered there.

- Look for a statement of the group's purpose and its "ground rules." These should appear on the site's main (or "home") page.

- Look for an option that enables you to report to the moderators any post that you find objectionable.

- Use your own good judgment and common sense. If something doesn't feel right, if you don't feel safe, accepted or understood, trust your instincts, leave immediately and find another group.

Finding professional help

If you're more comfortable in the care-giving role or feel uneasy with sympathy, or if you see the need for counseling as a sign of weakness or of mental illness, you may be reluctant to seek the help of a professional counselor. It takes strength and courage to let yourself be cared for, and you need not bear your sorrow all alone.

Even if you're mourning in a normal, healthy way, it is wise to use all the resources available to help you recover your balance and put your life back together again. Sometimes friends and family may worry too much about you, get too involved in your personal affairs, or not be available to you at all. When it seems that support from family and friends is either too much or not enough, a few sessions with a bereavement counselor may give you the understanding and comfort you need.

Unlike friendship, a professional counseling relationship offers you the opportunity to relate to a caring, supportive individual who understands the grief process, doesn't need you to depend upon and will allow you to grieve without interference. Within the safety and confidentiality of a therapeutic relationship, you can share your intimate thoughts, make sense of what you're feeling and clarify your reactions. An effective bereavement counselor is knowledgeable about the mourning process, helps you feel understood, offers a witness to your experience, encourages you to move forward, fosters faith that you will survive, and offers hope that you will get through your grief successfully. If after two or three sessions, you don't sense your counselor has a good understanding of your grief process or doesn't seem like the person who can help you, feel free to try another counselor.

Seeing a bereavement counselor is appropriate if:

- You feel uncomfortable with yourself or find yourself unable to function normally.

- You have reactions from which you can get no relief, or over which you feel no control.

- You wonder if your responses are normal, or if they've gone on too long.

- You have thoughts or feelings that you feel guilty about or you're reluctant to share with anyone else.

Seek professional help immediately if:

- You feel no grief reaction at all after a major loss.

- You have a history of mental illness, drug, or alcohol abuse.

- You have few sources of support.

- You see life as hopeless and are feeling suicidal.

Individual bereavement counseling is available at no cost to individuals and families whose loved ones were patients of Hospice of the Valley. Please contact Bereavement Services for further information: 602.530.6970.

UNDERSTANDING DIFFERENT MOURNING PATTERNS IN YOUR FAMILY

Grief is a family affair. When one member of a family dies, the entire family is affected. It's as if an important link in the family chain is suddenly broken and lost, and everyone is locked in a struggle to find the missing link, to repair the broken chain. Everyone is mourning their own personal loss in their own unique way. Roles and responsibilities shift, relationships change, communication and mutual support among members may suffer. Over time, the family must identify what the roles and functions of the lost member were, decide whose job it will be to execute those duties now and learn how to compensate for their absence.

Further complicating the situation is the fact that men, women and children are very different from each other, not just in personality patterns that affect how they think, feel and behave, but also in how they mourn. When someone dies, they will not experience or express their reactions in the same way. Failure to understand and accept these different ways of mourning can result in hurt feelings and conflict between partners and among family members during a very difficult time. Although there is grief work to be done, behaviors can be misinterpreted, needs may be misunderstood, and expectations may not be met. Children and adults are all very different, one from another, with their own unique needs for expression and support.

Differing personality patterns among family members will affect how each one individually expresses, experiences and deals with grief. While we all have the capacity to react to loss in a variety of ways, personality research shows that there are three basic styles or patterns of mourning: instrumental, intuitive and dissonant. Typically, a person trusts and prefers one pattern of response over the other two and will behave accordingly.

Instrumental mourners experience and speak of their grief intellectually and physically. They are most comfortable with seeking accurate information, analyzing facts, making informed decisions and taking action to solve problems. Remaining strong, dispassionate and detached in the face of powerful emotions, they may speak of their grief in an intellectual way, thus appearing to others as cold, uncaring and without feeling.

Intuitive mourners experience a full, rich range of emotions in response to grief. Comfortable with strong emotions and tears, they are sensitive to their own feelings and to the feelings of others, as well. Since they feel strong emotions so deeply, they're less able to rationalize and intellectualize the pain of grief, and more likely to appear overwhelmed and devastated by it.

Dissonant mourners encounter a conflict between the way they experience their grief internally and the way they express it outwardly, which produces a persistent discomfort and lack of harmony. The "dissonance" or conflict may be due to family, cultural, or social traditions. Although their grief may be profound and strongly felt, they struggle to hide their true feelings in order to preserve the image they wish to project to the public. Others may condemn themselves and feel very guilty for not feeling whatever they think is expected of them to feel.

Like everyone else in our Western culture, men are saddled with certain stereotypes. *Real* men are supposed to be tough, confident, rational and in control, not only of themselves but of situations as well. *Real* men don't cry, aren't afraid of anything and would never be caught asking for directions, let alone for help. *Real* men know exactly what to do in a crisis, and they're strong enough to support the rest of the family, too. If they cry or otherwise express their emotions, such behaviors are considered to be signs of weakness. Add to these sex role stereotypes the assumption that, if a man's grief doesn't show or he doesn't express thoughts and feelings of grief the same way a woman ordinarily does (by crying or by openly sharing with others, for example), then he must not be grieving at all.

In general, men are more often instrumental mourners. When men suffer the loss of a loved one, they tend to put their feelings into action, experiencing their grief physically, rather than emotionally. They deal with their loss by focusing on goal-oriented activities, which activate thinking, doing and acting. Rather than endlessly talking about or crying over the person who died, for example, a man may throw himself into time-limited tasks, such as planting a memorial garden or writing a poem or eulogy. Such activities give a man not only a sense of potency and accomplishment as he enters his grief, but also a means of escaping it when the task is done. If a man relates the details of his loss to his closest male friends, it's likely to be around activities like hunting, fishing, sporting events and card games. Although a man may let himself cry in his grief, he'll usually do it alone, in secret, or in the dark.

Women, on the other hand, tend to be intuitive mourners. They have been socialized to be more open with their feelings. They may feel a greater need to talk with others who are comfortable with strong emotions and willing to listen without judgment. Unfortunately, while it may be more acceptable for women in our culture to be expressive and emotional, all too often in grief they're criticized for being too sentimental or overly sensitive.

Children and adolescents grieve just as deeply as adults, but depending on their cognitive and emotional development, they will experience and express their grief differently from the grown-ups around them. Moving in and out of grief is natural for youngsters, and the symptoms of grief may come and go, varying in intensity. Their responses will depend on the knowledge and skills available to them at the time of the loss. Having had less prior experience with crisis and its consequences, their repertoire of coping skills is simpler, their capacity to confront the reality of loss more limited and their ability to find meaning in life's crises less mature. If surprised or embarrassed by the intensity of their grief, they may try to hide it or disguise it. Parents, relatives, teachers and friends are wise to watch and to tune in to their children and adolescents, to listen to them, be there for them and if unsure what's going on, to ask! More than anything else, children need their parents and the other adults in their world to be honest with them. They need accurate, factual information; freedom to ask questions and express their feelings; inclusion in decisions, discussions and family commemorative rituals; stable, consistent attention from their caretakers; and time to explore and come to terms with the meaning of their loss.

The way we mourn is as individual as we are, and our own gender biases may influence how we "read" another gender's mourning. Some females may be instrumental in pattern and style, and will mourn in traditionally "masculine" ways, and some males may be more intuitive by nature, and therefore express their grief in traditionally "feminine" ways. Regardless of differences in personality, gender and age, the pressures of grief are still present for all family members, and the tasks of mourning are the same: to confront, endure and work through the many effects of the death, so the loss can be dealt with successfully. Grief must be expressed and released in order to be resolved, and all family members need encouragement to identify and release emotions, to talk about and share their thoughts and to accept help and support from others.

Suggestions for coping with different mourning patterns:

If the mourner is an adult:

- Understand that our own personality and gender biases may influence how we "read" another person's mourning.

- What looks like inappropriate behavior may be an instrumental mourner's way of avoiding feelings or displaying emotions publicly. People should not be judged for how they are mourning.

- Instrumental mourners often *appear* to be further along in the grieving process than they actually are. Even if a person appears to be all right, it is unwise to make assumptions about what he or she is experiencing. When in doubt, *ask!*

- Those who turn to drugs or alcohol in an effort to numb their pain or break down their inhibitions need to know that, because alcohol is a depressant, it can add to the sadness they're already feeling. Distracting from the pain only delays the mourning process.

- Although men, women, adolescents and children mourn differently from one another, none of those ways is inappropriate.

- It is not helpful to take sides, supporting one way of mourning over another.

- The way we mourn is as individual as we are: some males mourn in intuitive, feeling, or more traditionally "feminine" ways, and some females mourn in instrumental, thinking, or more traditionally "masculine" ways.

- If someone seems more angry than sad at the death of a loved one, the individual may be angry at the situation, and anger may be the only way the person knows to express grief. It's useful in such cases not to take such anger personally, or to react defensively against it.

- Men are less likely to seek the support of others (either individually or in a group) in order to express (think, talk, cry, or write about) their feelings, especially if they don't feel respected, or if they find certain aspects of grief to be embarrassing. A man needs encouragement to share his reactions and emotions, to explore what his loved one's death means to him and to acknowledge how the loss affects his life.

If the mourner is a child:

- Recognize that death and loss are natural parts of living. Shielding children from grief is futile and gives them no role models to learn healthy, normal coping behaviors.

- Be open and meticulously honest. Children know when adults are shading the truth. If children discover that you've distorted the truth or lied to them, they'll have a great deal of trouble trusting you again.

- First find out what the children already know or think they know about dying and death.

- Validate feelings and encourage children to share their thoughts, fears and observations about what has happened.

- Offer explanations that are age appropriate and at the child's level of understanding. A child under age five needs comfort and support, rather than detailed explanations, whereas a child over age five needs information that is simple, accurate, plain and direct.

- Explain that in the circle of life, all living things will die someday and that death causes changes in a living thing.

- Help children understand what "dead" means (that the body stops working and won't work anymore) and that death is not the same as sleeping (that the sleeping body is still working, but just resting).

- Don't use confusing or misleading euphemisms such as "passed away," "lost," or "gone on." Such phrases imply the one who died is on a trip and will return, leave children feeling rejected or abandoned, or encourage them to go searching for the individual or hold out hope for his or her return.

- Explain how we might feel when someone dies: sad, mad, or confused, and we may cry sometimes. Let your children know that laughing and playing are still okay, too, and that you respect their need to be children at this sad and difficult time.

- Relieve the child of any feelings of responsibility for the death; magical thinking may lead a child to conclude that something she or he did, wished or imagined somehow caused the death.

- Avoid telling children that the dead person was so good or so special that God wants him or her to be with Him in heaven. Children may become angry with God or fear that they (or you) will be chosen next.

- Respect and encourage your children's needs to express and share feelings of sadness. When you bring up the subject, you're showing your own willingness to talk about it. When in doubt about your children's thoughts and feelings, ask.

- Don't feel as if you must have all the answers; sometimes just listening is enough. Expect that young children will ask and need answers to the same questions over and over again.

- Find and read some of the many wonderful stories and books written especially for children to help them better understand death and grief.

- Don't cut off their feelings by noting how well your children are handling their grief or how brave or strong they are. Let them see you upset and crying, which implies that it's all right to cry for those we love and lose.

- Children and adolescents may be reluctant to express their thoughts and feelings verbally. Encourage them to express their grief and preserve their memories in a variety of ways, including art, music, journal writing, story-telling and picture collecting.

- Let children and adolescents plan and participate in commemorative family rituals.

If the mourner is an adolescent:

- Recognize that teens are already struggling with the enormous physical and psychological changes and pressures of adolescence. No longer children, but not yet mature adults, they still need adult supervision, guidance and consistent, compassionate support.

- Don't deprive teens of their own need to mourn by pressuring them to "be strong" in support of a surviving parent, younger siblings, or other family members.

- Understand that teens don't like to stand out and feel different from their friends; they want to belong and normally turn to one another for support. But if a teen's friends have never experienced the death of a loved one, it's unlikely that they can fully understand what the bereaved adolescent is feeling or experiencing. Grieving teens do best when they're helped to connect with other teens who have also experienced a death.

- Assure adolescents that conflict in relationships between teens and adults is a normal part of growing up, and offer them every opportunity to vent their feelings about their relationship with the person who died. Teens striving to separate from authority figures and find their own identity normally feel somewhat alienated from parents, siblings and other family members, and if a loved one dies during this turbulent time, they can be left with feelings of guilt and unfinished business.

- Give teenagers permission not to be grieving all the time. If they've expressed their feelings and talked about the loss with others (family, friends, teachers and other helpers), it may not be useful for them to focus further on their loss. It's not disloyal of them to want to put their grief aside and enjoy life again.

- Be on the alert for signs that a teen may need extra help (depression, drastic changes in sleeping or eating habits, falling grades, substance abuse, sexual acting out, deteriorating relationships with family and friends).

- Children and adolescents will cope only as well as the adults around them. Helping yourself will help your children.

- Alert significant adults in your child or adolescent's life (family doctor, teachers, school counselor, caregivers, neighbors, relatives, friends) about the death in your family. Ask their help in keeping a watchful eye on your youngster, and ask for their additional support and understanding during this difficult time.

- Consider enrolling your child or adolescent in one of the children/family bereavement support groups offered by Hospice of the Valley, or by other agencies in the community. Call Bereavement Services for further details: 602.530.6970.

SETBACKS, AFTERSHOCKS AND THE RECURRENCE OF GRIEF

Setbacks are the unexpected, but inevitable, frustrations and disappointments you'll encounter in your efforts to rebuild following your loss. They can affect you physically, mentally, emotionally and spiritually. They include statements from family members or friends which, intentionally or not, discourage your efforts. They can be your own *internal* thoughts, feelings and attitudes, which have inhibited and debilitated you in the past: rigidity, closed-mindedness, self-doubt, bitterness, anger, disappointment and the temptation to quit. Or they can be *external* roadblocks stemming from natural occurrences or from bureaucratic rules and regulations you'll encounter along the way.

Aftershocks or "grief bursts" happen when some of the "down" feelings you've already experienced in grief come at you again several months after the death, or even after a year or more. Sometimes, something acts as a trigger and catches you by surprise: a song, a place, a movie or a season, and it's as if you're confronted with the death for the first time, all over again. Painful emotions crash in on you, and it feels as if you're starting the entire grief process anew.

Recurrence of grief is common and normal, but disturbing nonetheless. Although the strong feelings of grief are not continuous, they can return at any time, whenever you are reminded of your loss. They may be especially apparent toward the end of your first year, as you approach the anniversary date of your loved one's death.

As this special date draws near, you may find yourself preoccupied with thoughts of your loved one's diagnosis, treatment and care, remembering your experience of facing a terminal illness together. You may be frightened and confused, all this time expecting that your grief would have been resolved by now and finding instead that if anything, your pain has intensified.

Rest assured that what you're feeling is normal and to be expected. You are not losing ground; the progress you've made is real. Getting past this anniversary is but another significant step in finding your way through grief. At this point, it is only natural to look back and reflect on what used to be before you can let go of it, move on through your grief and embrace whatever your life is going to be in the future.

Some mourners make the mistake of measuring the depth of their love by the depth of their pain. They convince themselves that letting go of the pain of loss is the same as letting go of (and forgetting) their loved one. Letting go of what used to be is not an act of disloyalty, and it does not mean forgetting your lost loved one. You will never forget, because a part of the one who died remains in you. There are many things you can do to ensure that your loved one will be remembered, and to give testimony to your continuing relationship with that person. Letting go means leaving behind the sorrow and pain of grief and choosing to go on, taking with you only those memories and experiences that enhance your ability to grow and expand your capacity for happiness.

Suggestions for coping with setbacks, aftershocks and recurrence of grief:

- Accept that setbacks are a reality of life over which you have no control. Remember that, although you cannot choose what life has to offer, you can always choose how to respond. The attitudes you bring to life's circumstances are always within your control. You can choose to give up and give in, or you can choose to take charge of your life and keep moving forward.

- Know that aftershocks of grief are normal, and they will pass more quickly each time you experience them. They can be controlled somewhat by controlling the reminders of your loss, either by disposing of them or deliberately seeking them out. Maintain a balance between what you hold onto and what you let go of. Keep what's special or of sentimental value and when you're ready, discard the rest.

- Handle your memories with care. If they are painful and unpleasant, they can be hurtful and destructive. If they create longing and hold you to the past, they can interfere with your willingness to move on. You can choose which parts of life you shared that you wish to keep and which parts you want to leave behind.

- Soothe your pain by thinking of happy, as well as sad, memories. The happiness you experienced with your loved one belongs to you forever. Hold onto those rich memories, and give thanks for the life of the person you've lost, instead of brooding over the last days.

- Build a memory time into the day, or pack an entire day with meaning. It's easier to cope with memories you've chosen than to have them take you by surprise. Immerse yourself in the healing power of remembrance. Go to a special place, read aloud, listen to a favorite song. Celebrate what once was and is no more.

- Know that oftentimes, the anticipation of an anniversary date is worse than the actual day.

- Identify those days, events and seasons that are likely to intensify and rekindle your pain, and build comfort and healing into them. Plan what you're going to do ahead of time, even if you plan to be alone. Don't set yourself up for a bad day.

- Let your friends and relatives know in advance which days and events are significant for you. Verbalize your needs and include them in your plans. They may be very willing to help, but need for you to tell them how.

- If you're feeling anxious, confused or immobilized as a certain date or time approaches, get the reassurance you need by returning to your support group or speaking with your bereavement counselor.

- As this first year draws to a close, plan a memorial ritual. Draw on those familiar, comforting ceremonies and activities unique to your religion, culture, traditions, family or way of life. Use this ritual as your rite of passage through grieving to healing, to mark a shift in the way you mourn, or as an official end to this first year of mourning.

- Understand that you're never really finished with loss when someone significant leaves you. This loss will resurface during key developmental periods for the rest of your life. You will have to face it again and again, not as the person you are today, but as the person you will have grown to be in two or five or 20 years from now. Each time you will face it on new terms, but it won't take as long and it won't be as difficult.

COPING WITH HOLIDAYS AND OTHER CELEBRATION DAYS

Living with loss is challenging enough, but it can be especially difficult when families gather together to celebrate special occasions, such as birthdays, anniversaries, weddings, reunions, graduations, baptisms, bar mitzvahs, confirmations and traditional holidays.

When your loved one dies, you grieve not only for that person, but also for the life you used to have, the love the person gave you and all the special times you spent together. Perhaps there is no time of the year when you're more aware of the empty space your dear one has left behind than during the winter holiday season. Other days can be difficult, as well, depending on the memories you've attached to them: Valentine's Day, Mother's Day, Father's Day, Memorial Day, Labor Day, Independence Day, a birthday, or any other day that was particularly special to you. On such days, it may seem to you as if there is no room for celebration; there is only grief.

Holidays and other celebration days can create feelings of dread and anxiety in those who are bereaved. The clichéd images of family togetherness and the often unrealistic expectations of a day or season filled with picture-perfect, joyful gatherings can cause tremendous stress for those who are *not* grieving, let alone for those in the midst of the painful, isolating experience of loss. Holidays by nature are filled with nostalgia and tradition, but in grief, even the happiest memories can hurt.

When you're in the midst of pain, and the rest of the world wants to gather, give thanks and celebrate, you need to find ways to manage your pain and get through the day or the season with a minimum of stress. If you decide to do so, you can choose to embrace a holiday, or any other celebration day, as a special day on which to commemorate your loved one and to celebrate your love for that person. Death ends a life, but it does not end the relationship you have with the one who has died. The bonds of love are never severed by death, and the love you shared will never die, either. On any special day, you can find a way to commemorate and honor your loved one, to show that your love is eternal, even if you decide to do so in a very private and personal way.

Suggestions for coping with holidays and other celebration days:

- Have a family meeting. List all the things you ordinarily do for the holidays (sending greeting cards, decorating the house, stringing outdoor lights, putting up a tree, holiday baking, entertaining business associates, buying something special to wear, going to parties, visiting friends, exchanging gifts, preparing a big meal, etc.). Decide together what's important to each of you, what you want to do this year, what you can let go of and what you can do differently. For each task on the list, ask yourself these questions: Would the holidays be the holidays without doing this? Is this something I really want to do? Do I do it freely, or out of habit or tradition? Is it a one-person job, or can it be a group effort? Who's responsible for getting it done? Do I really like doing it?

- Do some things differently this year. Trying to recreate the past may remind you all the more that your loved one is missing. This year, try celebrating the holidays in a totally different way. Nothing is the same as it used to be, anyway. Go to a restaurant. Visit relatives or friends. Travel somewhere you've never gone before. If you decide to put up a tree, put it in a different location and make or buy different decorations for it. Hang a stocking in your loved one's memory, and ask each family member to express their thoughts and feelings by writing a note to, from or about your loved one, and place the notes in that special stocking for everyone to read. Buy a poinsettia for your home as a living memorial to your loved one for the holiday season.

- Do other things more simply. You don't have to discard all your old traditions forevermore, but you can choose to observe the holidays on a smaller scale this year.

- Take good care of yourself. Build time in your day to relax, even if you're having trouble sleeping. Eat nourishing, healthy meals, and if you've lost your appetite, eat smaller portions more frequently throughout the day. Sweet, sugary foods are everywhere, from Halloween until Easter, but too much sugar will deplete what little energy you have. Get some daily exercise, even if it's just a walk around the block. Avoid drinking alcohol, which intensifies depression and disrupts normal sleep.

- Just do it. We all know that we ought to think positively, eat right, exercise more and get enough rest, but grief robs us of the energy we need to do all those good and healthy things. Accept that in spite of what we know, it's often very hard to do what's good for us—then do it anyway. Don't wait until you feel like doing it.

- Pay attention to yourself. Notice what you're feeling and what it is you need. Feelings demand expression, and when we acknowledge them and let them out, they go away. Feelings that are stuffed don't go anywhere; they just fester and get worse. If you need help from others, don't expect them to read your mind. It's okay to ask for what you need. Besides, doing a favor for you during the holidays may make them feel better, too. Be patient and gentle with yourself, and with others as well.

- Expect to feel some pain. Plan on feeling sad at certain moments, and let the feelings come. Experience the pain and tears, deal with them, then let them go. Have faith that you'll get through this and that you will survive.

- Seek support from others. Grieving is hard work, and it shouldn't be done alone. You need to share your experience with someone who understands the pain of your loss. If your spouse, relative or friend cannot be the source of that support, you can find it elsewhere. Contact Bereavement Services at Hospice of the Valley (602.530.6970) for information on holiday and other special focus support groups offered throughout the Valley.

- Give something of yourself to others. As alone as you may feel in your grief, one of the most healing things you can do for yourself is to be with other people, especially during the holidays. Caring for and giving to others will nourish and sustain you and help you to feel better about yourself. If you can bring yourself to do so, visit someone in a nursing home, or volunteer your time at your church or synagogue. Do whatever you can, and let it be enough.

CREATING PERSONAL GRIEF RITUALS

Personal grief rituals are those loving activities that help us remember our loved ones and give us a sense of connectedness, healing and peace. Creating and practicing personal grief rituals also can help us release painful situations and unpleasant memories, freeing us to make our memories a positive influence in our lives. The ideas presented here are as unique and as varied as the people who invented them; think of ways that you can adapt them and make them your own. You are limited only by your own imagination. (See also *Memorials ~ Funerals ~ Rituals,* at www.griefhealing.com/memorials-funerals-rituals.htm.)

Suggestions for creating personal grief rituals:

- If you're a writer, *write.* It could be an article, an anecdote, a story, a poem, a song, a letter, an obituary, or a eulogy. If you don't want to write for someone else, keep a private journal and write about your feelings as you journey through your grief.

- Buy a very special candle, decorate it and light it in honor of your loved one.

- Purchase a book, perhaps a children's book, on coping with the loss of a loved one, and donate it to your local library or school. Ask the librarian to place a label inside the front cover inscribed "In memory of [your loved one's name]."

- Plant a tree, bush, shrub, garden, or flower bed as a permanent growing memorial to your beloved. Mark the site with a memorial plaque, marker, bench, or statue.

- Memorialize your beloved in cyberspace by lighting a virtual candle online, at http://www.gratefulness.org/candles/enter.cfm?l=eng.

- Write a special note, letter, poem, wish or prayer to your beloved; go outside, attach the paper to a balloon and let it go, or place it in a vessel and burn it, and watch the smoke rise heavenward.

- If you are harboring bad feelings or regrets, gather symbols to represent those hurtful or painful situations, events, or feelings from your past, place them in a container and hold a private burial or burning ceremony, saying goodbye and releasing them as you do so.

- Ask relatives, friends, co-workers and neighbors to gather their contributions, and put together a scrapbook or box of memories containing mementos, letters and photographs of your loved one.

- Celebrate the life of your loved one by continuing favorite traditions or eating favorite foods.

- Select a greeting card that you wish your beloved would have picked for you, and mail it to yourself.

- Give yourself a gift from your loved one that you always wished he or she would have given you, and think of your beloved whenever you use it or wear it.

Part Three
From Surviving to Transcending Your Grief

RECOGNIZING YOUR OWN PROGRESS

How do you know you're making progress in your mourning? Remember that change isn't always obvious and dramatic; it is a process that takes place over time. The grief experience is different for everyone; it doesn't happen all at once or at the same rate of speed. And unless you're aware of the clues to recovery and their significance, your progress through grief may be so subtle and so gradual that you will not notice it at all.

If you can recognize certain changes in attitudes, feelings and behaviors in yourself, you can measure your own progress through grief. Become aware of your own healing. Notice when you are able to:

- Drive somewhere by yourself without crying the entire time.

- Get through a day without feeling tired all the time.

- Concentrate on a book, movie, or television program.

- Not think of your loved one for a period of time, however brief.

- Get through a few hours or days nearly free of pain.

- Return to a daily routine.

- Eat, sleep and exercise normally again.

- Participate in a religious service without crying.

- Accept invitations.

- Listen to music you both loved without crying.

- Be more aware of the pain and suffering of others around you.

- Be more patient with yourself and with others.

- Notice others in like circumstances, and recognize and accept that loss is a common experience.

- Reach out to another in a similar situation.

- Realize that the sometimes thoughtless comments of others stem from ignorance, not malice.

- Find something to be thankful for.

- Be patient with yourself through grief attacks.

- Feel confident again.

- Accept things as they are without trying to recapture the way they used to be.

- Think less about the past.

- Look forward to the day ahead of you.

- Reach out to the future less fearfully.

- Stop and notice life's little pleasures, the splendor of creation and the beauty in nature.

- Catch yourself smiling and laughing again.

- Feel comfortable spending time alone.

- Remember your loved one less idealistically, as less perfect, with more human than saintly qualities.

- Review both pleasant and unpleasant memories without being overcome by them.

- Reinvest the time and energy once spent on your loved one.

- Remodel your space: rearrange furniture, change colors and textures of walls.
- Re-make your image: change your hairstyle, make-up or clothing.
- Explore new foods, new places and new things.
- Feel more in control of your emotions and less overwhelmed by them.
- Feel freer to choose when and how to grieve.
- Talk about your loss more easily.
- Feel less preoccupied with yourself and your loss.
- Feel a renewed interest in giving love and receiving it.
- Look back and see your own progress.
- Notice that time doesn't drag as much; the weekends aren't as long.
- Notice that the good days outnumber the bad, mood swings aren't as wide, time between upsets is greater.
- Plan the future more effectively.
- Think more clearly and feel more in control of your life.
- Make decisions and take responsibility for the consequences.
- Feel open to new and healthy relationships while maintaining old ones.
- Discover abilities in yourself you haven't developed before or didn't even know you had.
- Fill some of the roles once filled by your loved one or find others who can fill them.
- Recognize that loss has played an important part in your life and that growth can be a positive outcome.
- Identify how this experience has changed you for the better: what you've learned, what you've become and how you've grown.
- Share the lessons you have learned through loss with others.

RECOGNIZING WHO YOU ARE NOW

As you continue to come to terms with the impact of this loss on your life, you may notice your focus shifting from why this death happened to how you have grown through this experience to become a stronger person. With some satisfaction, you'll look back on all the new tasks you've mastered, the new roles you've had to fill, the changes you've endured (some of which may have been enormous, such as learning to live alone, rearing your children by yourself, or managing your own finances for the first time in your life) and recognize how you've grown. As you ponder where you've been, where you are now and what needs to happen next, you may see a whole new you looking back at you in the mirror— someone who's stronger, kinder and wiser than the person you once were.

FINDING MEANING IN YOUR LOSS

It is difficult to imagine surviving grief, much less transcending it. How do you triumph over sorrow when it seems as if your pain will never end?

When you confront the lessons of grief, you opt for surviving and transcending the pain. If you choose to do so, you can look at the pain of loss as having a specific purpose. Turning crisis into opportunity, you can find emotional and spiritual peace. You have a choice: you can either give up and withdraw into your tragedy, or you can grow from the experience. You can either succumb to the pain, or decide to transform yourself. The choice to grow, to transform the self, is not an easy one. It requires work, perseverance and endurance. Like everything else in grief, it is a process, but it is what makes loss worth surviving.

Chances are that you would trade everything you could ever gain in a heartbeat, if only that would bring your loved one back. But that is not an option. The only viable alternative is to make this pain count for something.

All that happens to us in life is material for our own growth. The death of a loved one can be a turning point that alters our perspective on life.

It is an opportunity to re-think, to question, to doubt who we were, what we thought we believed, how we used to live and how we ordered our priorities. It is a chance to find meaning in our loss.

There are many lessons to be learned from grief. Losing someone you love teaches you to:

- Stop, examine and appreciate what really matters, what's important, what's truly valuable in life.

- Live fully in the present, knowing that the past is gone and the future is not yet here.

- Appreciate the value and wonder of every precious moment, without taking any one of them for granted.

- Accept the freedom and joy of spontaneity, to play, to relax and to have fun.

- Find valuable insights buried in the give and take of daily life, to slow down, daydream and fantasize.

- Simplify your life, so you have more time and energy to share with those you love.

- Accept what's happened to you, roll with the changes and keep on growing, believing that you'll make it.

- Be patient with yourself, allowing the grieving process to happen in whatever way it will.

- Keep and develop your connections with others, knowing that you are not alone.

- Share your thoughts and feelings with others openly and honestly, and sooner rather than later.

- Rethink your attitude toward death as a natural part of the cycle of life.

- Be grateful for the love you shared, however briefly, and appreciate what you have left.

- Define yourself as a survivor, rather than a victim.

SHARING WHAT YOU'VE LEARNED WITH OTHERS

At some point in your grieving process, you may feel the need to channel your pain, as well as the time and energy once devoted to your relationship with your loved one, into something productive and meaningful. As one who truly understands the grieving process, you may feel ready to reach out to others who are suffering the pain of loss. Now that you've found your own way through the first year of grief, you have a great deal to share with other grievers: you can identify with their struggles, empathize with their sorrows and doubts and offer valuable information and support.

Hospice of the Valley was founded by volunteers, and to this day, volunteers at Hospice of the Valley are considered vital members of the team. Volunteers in Bereavement Services assist staff members with office tasks, special projects, sending condolence cards and preparing bulk mailings. Through periodic telephone calls over a 13-month period following the death, they offer compassion, understanding and support, as well as referrals to appropriate resources, to bereaved individuals whose family members were Hospice of the Valley patients. If you are interested in learning more about volunteer opportunities at Hospice of the Valley, you are encouraged to contact Bereavement Services: 602.530.6970.

LIVING PRODUCTIVELY AFTER YOUR LOSS

As you have learned by now, grief changes you. When you lose someone you love, you will never be the same as you were before. But within every sorrowful situation, growth is possible. Over time, you learn that although a part of you has died, another part is being reborn, making you stronger and more capable. As your energy is renewed and your strength is restored, you can move from withdrawal into healing. It is more than survival; it's a willingness to grow because of what you have lost. It is choosing to become something more than you were before. For example, because this loss has happened, you may find yourself choosing to be:

- More adventurous, more curious, less fearful and more willing to take risks.

- More loving and compassionate toward others.

- More appreciative of life and more grateful for the blessings of each day.

- More spiritually aware, seeing life in a larger context, with a greater purpose and feeling more connected to a higher power or divine spirit.

Finding your way through grief is like emerging from the safety of a cocoon to begin the continuation of a new life in a different, unfamiliar form. Such a transformation takes courage, effort and struggle, and it doesn't happen all at once. Like everything else in this grieving process of yours, it is something that happens at last.

Part Four
Helping Another in Grief

BEING WITH THOSE WHO MOURN

If you're like many other good-hearted, well-meaning people, you may find it difficult to *be there* for someone who is anticipating or coping with the death of a loved one. When you aren't sure what to say or do to support another person, it's natural to feel awkward and uncomfortable. It's not that you don't care or don't want to be helpful; it's just that you feel completely helpless in the face of loss and so does the person you want to help. You cannot take the mourner's pain away, and you cannot answer the question, "Why?" You cannot bring back the person who died, or restore the health of the person who is dying, and your friend cannot make you feel better by seeming to be helped. This is especially difficult if you've never been around people in mourning before, or if you've had no prior experience with deep grief in your own life. Another person's death may remind you of your own past losses, or of those that you also must face one day. It's hard to confront the fact that at some point, death will take your own loved ones, too, and that eventually you also will die. Feeling awkward and uncomfortable in the face of such realities is understandable.

REQUIREMENTS FOR HELPING ANOTHER IN GRIEF

You will need sufficient time, patience, perseverance, flexibility, optimism, understanding, warmth and compassion. If you think you do not qualify, consider this: You are only human, and those who are struggling in grief need someone who can identify with them, someone who won't judge them, someone as human as they are. While you may not know what to *say*, there still is plenty that you can *do*. And because you are only human, do only what you can, and let it be enough. If you're a member of a family in mourning, give yourself permission to not always *be there* for other family members. Be good to yourself. Take a break if and when you need it, and seek some outside social and/or spiritual support or personal grief counseling. The best way to take care of another's grief is to take care of your own grief first.

WHEN THE MOURNER IS A CHILD

Remember that anyone old enough to love is old enough to grieve. Do what you can to give children special attention. Create quiet time for talking. Let them know you're sad about the death and would be glad to talk with them about it, if and when they want to.

WHEN SOMEONE IS MOURNING THE LOSS
OF A BELOVED PET

Acknowledge the person's pain as legitimate and real, no different from that of losing a cherished friend or special family member. Recognize that only your friend knows the heartfelt place that was occupied by a special animal companion, and only your friend can measure just how much has been lost.

WHAT MOURNERS NEED FROM US

In the aftermath of the death of a loved one, especially in the beginning, mourners are very susceptible to disappointments and vulnerable to others' insensitivity. They need emotional support to help alleviate suffering and help to be in the world in new and different ways.

If those left behind are to heal through grief, they must also *mourn*— that is, they need to express their grief (thoughts, feelings) *outwardly.* Over the weeks and months following the death, they must accept the harsh reality that someone they loved has died and will never physically be present to the mourner again. Pushing away some of this reality at times is normal; mourners will embrace it in manageable doses as they are ready. Allowing the pain in all at once is overwhelming. In general, mourners need someone who:

- Is present.
- Offers to be there in a helpful, loving, supportive, respectful and non-judgmental way.
- Can actively demonstrate caring and concern.
- Will bear witness to the struggle.
- Is with and will continue to be with the mourner.
- Will honor the person's unique journey through grief.
- Is sensitive to cultural, ethnic, religious and family traditions.
- Helps maintain the person's physical health and emotional equilibrium.

SUGGESTIONS FOR HELPING ANOTHER IN GRIEF

Information included here stems from professional knowledge and skills, from insights gained through personal experience with loss, and from companioning many others who have faced losses of their own. If any of these ideas don't fit with a particular culture or tradition, or if they don't seem to suit you or those you're wanting to help, then simply ignore them and go on to others.

First, learn about the grief experience, and let go of some of the harmful myths you may have heard about grief and healing. (See *Part One: Understanding the Grief Process.*) Don't assume that the person who seems to be experiencing little pain is "doing well" with grief. Take some time to review your own personal experiences of death and grief, recalling who died, what was helpful and not helpful to you, and how you felt about it.

What you can do immediately after the death:

- Acknowledge the loss. Either in person, by telephone or in writing, let the mourner know who you are, how you became aware of the loss and that you care.

- Attend the funeral. Say goodbye to the deceased and demonstrate support for those most impacted by the death. If possible, attend the visitation, funeral, committal and gathering afterward.

- Let the mourner know if you found the ceremony especially meaningful.

- Assemble a funeral scrapbook for the family, which could include the obituary, funeral program and room for cards, notes and other mementos.

- Arrange to have the ceremony video- or audio-taped. Offer to review the recording with the mourner at a later time.

- Offer tangible symbols of support: a phone call, note, letter, dish of comfort food, flowers or a potted plant, a hope-filled book, or a photo frame.

- Send flowers, a potted plant, hanging basket, bulbs, tree seedling or perennials to place or plant at the grave site.

- Contact the mourner's network of friends and family and help them choose a way to help (e.g., check on the mourner, fix a meal, walk the dog, cut the grass, rake the leaves).

- Fix and bring a meal. Include non-alcoholic, non-caffeinated beverages.

- Initiate contact. Invite the mourner to share what happened, with ample opportunity to tell you the story of the loss.

- Listen with your heart, with honest concern and curiosity, respectfully and without judging, without criticism, without giving advice, without being the expert with all the answers.

- Encourage, reflect, respond to and validate feelings, however they are expressed, and hold them in confidence.

- Be willing to listen to the same story, over and over again if needed, with mouth closed and ears open.

- Be fully and physically present: Allow sufficient time; listen attentively; don't appear rushed; sit rather than stand; maintain eye contact and an attentive posture with your arms free and uncrossed; match the volume, tone and speed of your voice to the mourner's; let the mourner steer the conversation; nod and affirm.

- Accept, permit and be present in times of silence.

- Permit yourself to cry, too. Your tears mingled with your friend's convey what words cannot.

- Understand the uniqueness of grief. Everyone is different, shaped by our own individual life experiences.

- Be patient. The grief process takes a long time. Let the mourner set the pace.

- Recognize that although you cannot take the pain away, you can enter into it with your friend. You can remain available long after the death occurs, when the mourner will need you the most.

What you can do over time:

Help the mourner to absorb the reality of the loss and its consequences:

- Empower your friend to identify which activities, tasks and commitments can be given up or set aside for now, to avoid feeling so overwhelmed.

- Create safe places to mourn that fit your friend's personality. Find appropriate forms of expression (talking, writing or making music).

- Keep the focus on the mourner's grief, not on your own story of loss.

- Allow exploration, searching for meaning and questioning the purpose of life and death, without supplying answers or imposing your own spiritual beliefs.

- Listen to and honor the mourner's religious beliefs.

- If it fits with your belief, pray for your friend. Place the mourner's name on a prayer list at church or in an online prayer circle. Bring your friend into your consciousness, think about and hold the person in your heart and soul for a little while each day.

Help the mourner experience and express the feelings of grief:

- Spend time together weekly. Commit to contacting your friend. Schedule regular, ongoing contact time and note it in your calendar.

- Accept the person as is, without judgment or reproach.

- Allow for differences in grief. Walk beside the mourner, not behind or in front.

- Accept the ups and downs, tolerate the ambiguities, have faith in the process.

- Expect a multitude of emotions, which are normal and healthy, including numbness, anger, guilt, fear, confusion, relief and exhaustion. Don't think you need to change them.

- Expect occasional "grief bursts" (sudden upsurges of grief); allow feelings of sorrow.

- Allow crying in your presence, without offering a tissue or a hug (which may stifle the tears).

- Offer gentle and appropriate touch, but only if the person wants to be touched or hugged, and make it easy for the mourner to move away if that's what is preferred.

- Encourage the mourner to take some time off from grieving, to do or think about something else for a while.

- Bring the gift of music. It soothes the soul, nurtures the spirit and puts the mourner in touch with feelings, both happy and sad.

- Spend time near the water (a river, a lake, or the ocean) or the sound of water (a fountain). Give the mourner a tabletop fountain from a home, patio, or garden store.

- Gaze at the stars and ponder the universe together, either outside with a telescope at night, or at a planetarium.

Help the mourner adjust to new circumstances:

- Encourage self-care: regular medical and dental check-ups.

- Present your friend with certificates for self-indulgent gifts: day spa, massage, facial, manicure, pedicure, haircut or a shave.

- Be a stand-in handy person. Help with daily chores or tasks that once belonged to the person who died.

- Without offending or shaming the person, look around, and do whatever needs doing. Run errands, get groceries, offer to be a chauffeur to an appointment.

- Be a stand-in partner for activities formerly enjoyed with the one who died, such as playing golf or shopping.

- Rent a movie to watch together, or take the mourner to a movie and discuss it together afterward.

- Mark your calendar to remember those special life event days: the birthday and death day of the person who died, anniversaries and holidays.

- Encourage the mourner to plan ahead. Making plans in advance of difficult days can alleviate some of the worries.

- Accompany your friend to the cemetery on Memorial Day, Veterans Day, Labor Day, Mother's Day, Father's Day; bring or help plant flowers at the grave site.

- Reach out at holidays. Invite the mourner to share them with you, take a trip with you, or accept a special gift from you.

- Expect sadness at landmark events and rites of passage (baptisms, bar mitzvahs, confirmations, proms, graduations, weddings, funerals), when the mourner is more acutely aware of the absence of the deceased.

- Encourage spending time with children (a school play, a day at the zoo).

- Consider your friend's interests and talents. Together visit neighborhood shops, restaurants, museums, guided tours, or art galleries. Enjoy a board or card game. Ask your friend to teach you something (cooking, gardening, sewing, scrapbooking) or sign up for a class in something you both want to learn. Help your friend find an enjoyable social group, suggest connecting with a sponsor from the group, or offer to join, too.

- Take a drive together to a scenic spot that may encourage conversation.

- Ease loneliness. Invite the mourner to your home for dinner, with a game or movie afterward. Suggest an overnight stay.

- Invite your friend to exercise with you (walking, biking, swimming, hiking, gardening or yoga).

- Encourage doing something daring, wild and free, such as river rafting, hang gliding, rock climbing, parasailing, or skydiving.

- Gently encourage the person gradually to begin socializing, to begin developing a new way of being with other people. Help to set up "safety nets" in advance (limiting the length of a visit, making arrangements for an easy departure by driving oneself, or sitting near the exit).

- Honor your friend's old identity (as a spouse, parent, sibling, or child), and notice the new one that is emerging. Recognize and comment on the positive changes you see: someone who is stronger, more caring, more appreciative, more tolerant, less judgmental.

- Acknowledge the importance of this person and how much your friendship matters to you.

Help the mourner regain a sense of control by understanding and normalizing what happens in grief:

- Find articles and books on grief (check the library, local or online bookstore, Compassion Books or Centering Corporation); consider journals, workbooks, poetry.

- Give a gift subscription to a healing magazine *(Grief Digest, Living with Loss),* or another periodical you think your friend would like.

- Help the mourner find helpful grief Web sites, such as GriefHealing.com.

- Look for workshops on grief, loss and bereavement open to the public and sponsored by hospice, The Compassionate Friends, AARP, mortuaries, churches and other community organizations.

- Suggest joining a support group, but don't insist or push, as your friend may not be ready. Contact Hospice of the Valley or your local hospice or funeral home for a support group schedule, and give it to your friend.

- Encourage your friend to join Hospice of the Valley's online Grief Healing Discussion Groups, at www.hovforum.ipbhost.com.

Help the mourner create a spiritual bond with the deceased loved one that defines the person as gone, but still available:

- Encourage active remembering of the one who died and commemoration of a life that was lived.

- Accept as normal and healthy your friend's efforts to maintain connection (and even communication with) the person who died.

- Use the name of the deceased. This helps recall the presence of the one who died and confirms that the person has not and will not be forgotten.

- Share your memories of the deceased loved one.

- Plan a ceremony of remembrance (light a candle, share memories), or construct a memory book (ask friends to write notes, share photos); make a quilt of the person's clothing.

- Give a tree as a gift, or organize a tree planting, and let your friend pick the spot.

- Find ways to mention the loved one's name in family rituals, conversations with family and friends, religious services, memorials and donations to charity.

Help the mourner to keep hope alive, believing that suffering can be overcome:

- Be sensitive to the timing of such assurances. Avoid offering too much too early, or too little too late.

- Convey your own hopeful attitude toward life and love.

- Share some personal experiences that radiate hope, offering what is appropriate for your friend and has been true for you.

- Remind your friend of past examples of perseverance and strength.

- Give specific feedback about how you see your friend making progress now.

- Offer encouragement with inspirational cards and other written messages.

- Share inspirational books, tapes, CDs, videos and DVDs.

- Find and share articles that apply to your friend's individual situation.

- Offer to hold your friend's hope yourself, willingly and lovingly, until the person is ready to hold it again one day.

Join with the mourner in the search for meaning:
Is there any meaning to be found in this loss? As your friend continues along this grief journey, you can help the person discover whatever lessons have been learned or identify what can be learned from this experience. Together you can talk over some questions that might bring some clarity to what has happened:

- What self-discoveries is your friend making?

- What personal qualities have been strengthened as a result of this experience?

- What strengths can be identified that were not apparent before?

- What is becoming of the person your friend used to be? Who is your friend now?

- What was important in your friend's life before this loss, compared to what is important now?

- How has this experience impacted your friend's values and spiritual beliefs?

- Does your friend see the world any differently now?

- What other "big questions" about life and love and loss can you think of to discuss?

ADDITIONAL RESOURCES

Hospice of the Valley Bereavement Services
Offers information, literature and reading lists; individual bereavement counseling at no cost to those whose family members were patients of Hospice of the Valley; listings of bereavement support groups sponsored by Hospice of the Valley, as well as by others in the community; online discussion groups and referral to appropriate resources. Contact Bereavement Services: 602.530.6970, hov.org.

Grief Digest Magazine

Features articles on coping and dealing with grief and help for the caregiver, by outstanding clinicians, writers and speakers in the field of grief intervention, as well as essays, stories and poems written by the bereaved. Write or call for writer's guidelines: *Grief Digest Magazine,* P. O. Box 4600, Omaha, NE 68104, 866.218.0101. On the Internet: griefdigest.com; e-mail: centeringcorp@aol.com.

Living with Loss Magazine

Originally created as a "support group in print" to serve the bereaved; offers hope and healing with timely articles, new publications and resources; emphasizes traditional and alternative perspectives and resources for healing the body, mind and spirit in grief. Includes regular departments written by professionals eminent in the field of grief education, and invites contributions from readers. Request writer's guidelines via e-mail. Bereavement Publications, Inc., P. O. Box 61, Montrose, CO 81402, 888.604.4673. On the Internet: livingwithloss. com; e-mail: grief@livingwithloss.com.

Centering Corporation

Non-profit organization dedicated to providing education and resources for the bereaved. Publishes *Grief Digest Magazine;* develops books and workshops on bereavement; offers free catalog with an extensive listing of grief literature categorized by topic (e.g., Children and Grief; Death of a Child; Death of a Parent; Men and Grief; Women and Grief; Pet Loss). Centering Corporation, 7230 Maple St., Omaha, NE 68134, 866.218.0101. On the Internet: centeringcorp.com; e-mail: centeringcorp@aol.com.

Grief Healing Discussion Groups

Safe, anonymous, online site where the bereaved can share stories of loss and ask questions to learn more about the normal grieving process. Sponsored by Hospice of the Valley; monitored and moderated by professional bereavement counselors. On the Internet: hovforum. ipbhost.com.

Grief Healing

Offers information, comfort and support to those coping with or anticipating the loss of a loved one, whether a person or a cherished animal companion. Includes useful articles on various aspects of loss, recommended
book lists, inspirational writings and poetry and categorized links to dozens of other helpful articles, books, Web sites and other resources. Developed and hosted by the author, a certified hospice bereavement counselor.
On the Internet: griefhealing.com; e-mail tousleym@aol.com.

SUGGESTIONS FOR FURTHER READING

It has been said that every grief needs a thousand tellings. When we are
stricken with grief over the loss of someone we love, whether that is a
special person in our lives or even a treasured companion animal, we
each will have our own stories to tell, as well as a need to know the
stories of others.

Whether written by experts in grief intervention, or ordinary people
who have found their own way through grief, today there are literally
dozens of excellent books on bereavement and loss, and they are readily
available to all of us.

Teachers, helpers, parents and children also can find and read a vast
assortment of stories and books written especially for children to help
them better understand the grief that accompanies dying, death and loss.

These wonderful sources of hope and healing are as near as the
bereavement section of your local library or neighborhood bookstore.
Hospice of the Valley maintains an extensive list of recommended
readings. Please call Bereavement Services for further information:
602.530.6970.

You also can browse through some of the hundreds of titles available on
the Internet. To find books I've read and personally recommend, see the
titles listed under the *Books* section on the *Articles ~ Columns ~ Books*
page of my *Grief Healing* Web site: http://www.griefhealing.com/articles-
columns-books.htm. For excerpts, reviews and purchasing information,
click on the book's title.

ABOUT THE AUTHOR

As both a bereaved parent and a bereaved child, Marty Tousley has focused her practice on issues of loss, grief and transition for more than 40 years. She joined Hospice of the Valley in Phoenix, Arizona, as a bereavement counselor in 1996, and now serves as moderator for its online *Grief Healing Discussion Groups, http://www.hovforum.ipbhost.com.* A frequent contributor to health care journals, newsletters, books and magazines, she has authored a number of books, booklets, articles and online e-mail courses addressing various aspects of loss and grief. With her special interest in grief and the human-animal bond, she facilitated a pet loss support group for bereaved animal lovers in Phoenix for 15 years, and now serves as consultant to the Pet Loss Support Group at Hospice of the Valley and to the Halton-Peel Pet Loss Support Group in Ontario, Canada. Her own *Grief Healing* Web site (griefhealing.com) offers information, comfort and support to anyone who is anticipating or coping with the loss of a loved one, whether a person or a cherished companion animal. She is certified as a Fellow in Thanatology (Death, Dying and Bereavement) by the Association for Death Education and Counseling and as a Clinical Specialist in Adult Psychiatric/Mental Health Nursing Practice by the American Nurses Association. Marty welcomes reader questions and comments; she can be contacted at tousleym@aol.com or through her Web site, GriefHealing.com.